Everyday STEWARDSHIP

LIVING AN EXTRAORDINARY LIFE

Tracy Earl Welliver, MTS

This book is dedicated to my wife, Mariann,
and my three children, Nathan, Sarah Kate, and Zachary.
You have sacrificed a good amount of time with Dad
due to my travel & responsibilities.
Thank you for your love and understanding.
I pray we continually grow closer to God together
and offer Him endless glory and praise.

Everyday Stewardship: Living An Extraordinary Life

Copyright ©2018 by LPi.
All rights reserved.

No part of this document may be reproduced or transmitted in any form or by any means, electronic, mechanical, photocopying, recording, or otherwise, without prior written permission of LPi.

Scripture texts in this work are taken from the *New American Bible, revised edition* ©2010, 1991, 1986, 1970 Confraternity of Christian Doctrine, Washington, D.C. and are used by permission of the copyright owner. All rights reserved. No part of the New American Bible may be reproduced in any form without permission in writing from the copyright owner.

ISBN: 978-0-940169-16-6

Cover design by Theresa Schiffer

To order contact:
LPi
2875 S. James Drive
New Berlin, WI 53151
(800) 950-9952 x2469

lpiconnections@4LPi.com
www.4LPi.com

Printed in the United States of America.

Contents

Acknowledgements

There is a single author name on any book, but any book represents a team effort.

THANK YOU to ...

Carin Winghart for your constant encouragement and always believing in me.

Julie Schnittka for an unbelievable amount of work on preparing and editing this book. I truly feel that this book is not mine but OURS.

Theresa Schiffer and the graphic design team, who turned my book into a real piece of art.

Michael Murphy for being a great companion on this journey of personal stewardship with me. It is an honor to work in the vineyard of our Lord with you.

My family for loving me and making my life meaningful.

The thousands of people I have met in the churches and dioceses in the past 3 years since the publication of the first book. Your willingness and desire to embrace the book and the Everyday Stewardship journey have humbled me to tears. We are one Body of Christ, and it is an honor and privilege to be part of that body with all of YOU.

Reflecting on the Journey

In the three years since the publication of "Everyday Stewardship: Reflections for the Journey," I have been blessed in so many ways it is hard to account for most of them. The response from those in the Church has been overwhelming. I am humbled and honored to have played even a little part in many a parish or diocesan journey of stewardship.

I have received many wonderful letters and emails from people who have been touched by the reflections. I continue to meet Stewardship Committee and Parish Council leaders who use the book for an opening reflection at every meeting. Parishes have formed Everyday Stewardship study/prayer groups. Some have had me come to speak to their community for a day or for an extended parish mission. It has been quite a spectacular experience.

However, the Everyday Stewardship journey has only begun! It is with great love that I share with you the next steps on this pathway. This volume provides you with 68 more reflections for your personal and communal journey. Like the first book, each reflection springs forth from a passage of Holy Scripture and ends with an idea for response and a reflection question. Doodle boxes accompany each reflection as well for you to write, scribble, or doodle in all you want. This is not meant to be a book that calls for a passive response. If you are moved by what you read, you should act!

The book is organized with eight general reflections, followed by 10 reflections for each of the 6 Characteristics of an Everyday Steward: Mindful, Prayerful, Grateful, Gracious, Committed, and Accountable. As an individual or with a group, you may want to journey with me for 10 weeks, reading a reflection from each characteristic 6 days in a row with a 7th day for rest. No matter how you use this book, hopefully there is enough here for you to be challenged and to discover new aspects of your spiritual journey.

Praying your "ordinary" becomes "extraordinary,"

Tracy E Welliver

Living an Extraordinary Life

You might not think of yourself or your life as being extraordinary. This type of experience might even seem light years away from your own reality. Why do you think this?

To be Christian, particularly Catholic, means that the supernatural is never that far away. Our faith attests to things like the communion of saints, sacraments, and sometimes, actual miracles. These are not realities debated on some ghost hunter show on cable television. We are talking real everyday life.

What part do you and I play in all of this? Are we not in communion with the saints? Do we not encounter the real Jesus Christ in the sacraments? Is there a greater miracle than Jesus coming to us under the disguise of bread and wine?

Jesus Christ has entered our lives and continues to be present to us so that we might draw closer to him and bring his Gospel to a world that needs it so badly. Our stewardship brings others into contact with the real Jesus. Others have a chance to see in us something that is actually supernatural. You can't get more extraordinary than that!

We are called by Christ to make the ordinary extraordinary. We are called to bring the supernatural into the natural world. We are everyday people called to live the Gospel within our everyday lives, making those lives then simply extraordinary.

Don't think for a second this is an overstatement. When you begin to see stewardship in all aspects of your life and strive to achieve complete surrender to God, all things are possible. You and I have been given much by God. The choice is now ours.

We Are All Called to Be Everyday Stewards

In the years since the first book, I have had the chance to talk to so many different people and to think about so many different aspects of the stewardship way of life, particularly in the light of the six characteristics. The Everyday Stewardship spirituality was never meant to replace or improve on anything. It simply was a way for ordinary people to more easily grasp the meaning of stewardship and to begin to live this way of life in all aspects of their lives, not just their church community.

If a philosophy, theology, or spirituality cannot be understood and applied to all people regardless of age, place of origin, education, or economics, I believe it cannot be called truth. Truth cuts through all barriers, labels, and experiences, touching people at their very core. Jesus is truth. His Gospel is truth. The life Jesus calls all of us to is a way to live out and provide testimony to that truth.

Although we are following a truth when committing ourselves to a stewardship way of life, it does not mean that we do not have a difficult time of it. Truth does not make the journey easier. It just makes it worthwhile.

All of us before God are sinners, falling short of the example set for us by Jesus Christ. As we mature in our faith, we do find ways to avoid some of the spiritual pitfalls along the way. However, not even maturity can chase away the temptations of the world.

In some ways, I have found three types of people who at times can struggle with stewardship more than most. Even though the groups are different, some of the same reasons for the struggle remain: a fear or inability to fully trust, a lack of awareness of their own God-given gifts and talents, and a greater focus on one's self. Just hearing about stewardship, or the 6 Characteristics of an Everyday Steward, can cause discomfort and concern.

The Young

When you are an adolescent, you are still in information-gathering mode about this world of ours. You are not sure whom to fully trust, and you are skeptical of many things that are told to you as "truth." You are also the center of your universe. That makes sense because you can't understand anything else out there unless you know yourself and are aware of how interactions with the forces around you benefit or hurt you.

That doesn't mean you are not generous. In fact, young people are constantly looking for ways to give. However, it is mainly with their friends or those they wish were friends. That's okay, because that is how we learn to be stewards. We give first to our family, then to our friends, then to those we do not know. Once we are more secure with the person God created us to be and we have at least a few friends with whom to share the journey, the world is wide open to our generosity.

I am no expert on young people. I once was young. I have had three children of my own. I have had my hand in various youth ministry groups over the course of two decades. However, I know of no magic answers when communicating to teens about stewardship and discipleship. That is because I believe there is no such thing as a collective group called *youth* who all exhibit the same characteristics and personalities. Young people come in all types and personalities, and no two are alike. We make a big mistake when we begin sentences with, "The youth of today..."

If we want to communicate stewardship spirituality in a way that makes sense, we need to address one's state in life. For most young people, this means looking at what it means to be a student. I sometimes share with people my "10 Points on Good Stewardship for Students," which you can download from the Coaching & Consulting section of the LPi website (www.4lpi.com.) Getting all people, including youth, to see that good stewardship encompasses all of their life is key. Stewardship is about so much more than activities in a church community. That's why it is called *a way of life!*

The Retired

By the time you reach retirement, you lived on this earth for many years and have given so much to family, work, and your parish. Now you find yourself retired from a job that took up most of your time for several decades. Perhaps you even worked the same job all those years. In many ways, it is all you know. You value time more now than ever, because you have more of it on a daily basis, but less of it in the big picture of life. You want to give of yourself, and different corners of your world are calling upon you, including your parish community.

What will you give and how will you give it? You either were in an occupation you are unsure lends itself well to other avenues of life, or you are just tired of the same thing and want to do something different. However, you are at a loss. Surely you have much to give but are unsure of all the gifts and talents you have or if they are inside you at all.

Our world is experiencing a huge growth in the senior population, and many of them have defined themselves by their career or family most of their adult lives. As Church, we have a responsibility to help them see themselves as God sees them: fearfully and wonderfully made with many different dimensions and unique gifts. It is no doubt that we see high rates of depression in the two groups mentioned here that have sometimes the greatest struggle with identity: the youngest and oldest among us.

Gift discernment programs in parishes provide useful information to all those who seek to serve their God more fully. Seniors, particularly the retired, can benefit greatly from seeing themselves as having more to give than they ever realized. It helps them see a larger purpose for their lives. It allows them to see they are an important part of the Body of Christ. When speaking to both youth and seniors, it is important that we communicate they not only need Jesus Christ, but his Church needs them.

Leaders

You find yourself either in a role that you have worked hard to achieve or one that simply seemed to fall into your lap. Either way, you feel the pressure of leading others. You are unsure whom to fully trust, and you want to be able to see positive results under your leadership.

You might fall into one of three different traps:

1. **You try to do everything yourself**. You know you can rely on yourself, and it is the quickest path to getting things done. Problem is, eventually you actually haven't led anyone anywhere. Instead, you have gotten things done, and everyone simply watched. Worse yet, you are about to burn out. You are a team of one!
2. **You try to lead like someone else**. You have role models, and you want to be just like them. The issue here is that you aren't made like those others. God made you like you. Instead of using what God gave you to lead, you try to use that which you do not have at all. You are now frustrated and wonder why you can't get people to follow you.
3. **You try to please everyone by being everything to everyone**. In the end, you find you are actually meaningless to most. You can't give to everyone in the same manner. Those you lead don't need the best person they think should lead them; they need the best leader you can give them.

Stewardship is about knowing the gifts and talents you have been given by God, cultivating them to an increase, and then giving them back to God and His people. A good leader knows what they have been given to be the best leader possible. While sharing their gifts with others, they also allow those around them to give freely of what they have to make a difference. The best leaders create well-rounded teams of people who rely on one another.

Good leadership is needed inside and outside of the Church. That being said, wouldn't it be great if the Church could show the world what good leaders look like? Stewardship spirituality can play a major role in making that possible. The 6 Characteristics of an Everyday Steward presented in this book provide some good places to start when trying to develop into a good leader.

1. Good leaders need to be **mindful** of all those around them. They need to be looking for the pathways that God is leading them into. They cannot be afraid of what happens next. They need to trust in God and allow Him to speak to them in the moments of everyday life.

2. A leader should always be open to mentoring. Jesus Christ is that mentor. By cultivating a **prayerful** life, Jesus is there at all times to assist. I think of a framed print that hangs in my office entitled, "The Servant." The picture is of a man in a suit at a large presidential-type desk, and he is turned in his chair so Jesus can wash his feet. Do you really want to lead anyone without having Jesus on your side? He comes to wash your feet so that you may be moved to wash the feet of those you serve.

3. We need to be **grateful** for all we have been given, the great and the small. Good leaders should give thanks for all that is provided to them and to the community or team they lead. Seeing the obvious gifts is easy. The ability to see those things that are not obvious but can have a great impact is a skill to be developed.

4. The world needs more **gracious** leaders! To lead others gracefully seems to be a lost art in many places. This need not be the case in the Church! The leader who can show hospitality rather than only expect it from others is one who draws followers to him or her.

5. A leader who is **committed** to a stewardship way of life while asking others to do the same is one I would want to follow. Our leaders need to be able to show resolve in the face of adversity and a willingness to fail. Risk is necessary for growth. However, even when we are open to risk, it is with a desire to stay the course and to correct the path if the journey goes off the intended road.

6. Finally, a leader who is willing to be held **accountable** is one who is able to gain the trust of those who follow. We should all be trying our best on this spiritual journey. But if we are not giving our best, our brothers and sisters should be able to point it out to us without fear. In fact, we need them to do so. This is how we all get to where we are going together.

And Now...

I finally offer to you this book with the same words from the previous book:

Thank you for considering embarking upon this journey. This might be a beginning for you or just another leg on an already powerful spiritual expedition. Either way, keep in mind that God is there every day in the smallest of life's moments. Together, as Everyday Stewards, let us strive to be better today than we were yesterday, and better tomorrow than we are today. Let us be mature disciples who respond daily to the call of Jesus. We will be transformed, and our parish communities will be transformed as well.

The Stewardship Journey

True Sacrifice

Jesus said to them, "Amen, amen, I say to you, unless you eat the flesh of the Son of Man and drink his blood, you do not have life within you. Whoever eats my flesh and drinks my blood has eternal life, and I will raise him on the last day. For my flesh is true food, and my blood is true drink. Whoever eats my flesh and drinks my blood remains in me and I in him. Just as the living Father sent me and I have life because of the Father, so also the one who feeds on me will have life because of me. This is the bread that came down from heaven. Unlike your ancestors who ate and still died, whoever eats this bread will live forever."

–John 6:53-58

When I was a child, I can remember stopping by my parish or another local Catholic church to just spend some time in prayer before the Holy Eucharist. We didn't have exposition and adoration much in those days, but we were keenly aware of the presence of Jesus in the tabernacle. I would sometimes stare at the lighted candle near it and know that Jesus was alive.

I had never heard someone speak about a stewardship way of life back then. If I am honest, the primary message I heard in those days was along the lines of "We need to be as good as we are able." Sacrifice was only at Lent, disciples were people in the Bible, and generosity mostly had to do with the collection basket and the poor box at the church entrance. I even went to Catholic schools!

Maybe the message of stewardship was there somewhere packaged differently and I just missed it. It wasn't until I was an adult, and after acquiring two theology degrees, that I understood both with my head and my heart what a stewardship way of life really meant. But I look back at those days and I realize that the groundwork was laid for me to understand these things. It was those times before the Holy Eucharist that I began to understand true sacrifice. It was at those times that I began to understand how actions and realities that seem so simple to the human eye can be so profound. And it was at those times that I began to see that true love knows no bounds.

IDEA FOR RESPONSE

If you can find the opportunity in a parish near you, set aside 15-30 minutes for Eucharistic Adoration.

TAKE TIME TO REFLECT

Jesus is truly present to us in the Holy Eucharist. Name 3 people you know who show the face of Christ to you by their sacrifice.

ADORATION

The Value of Your Stewardship

Jesus said to him, "I am the way and the truth and the life. No one comes to the Father except through me. If you know me, then you will also know my Father. From now on you do know him and have seen him." Philip said to him, "Master, show us the Father, and that will be enough for us." Jesus said to him, "Have I been with you for so long a time and you still do not know me, Philip? Whoever has seen me has seen the Father. How can you say, 'Show us the Father'? Do you not believe that I am in the Father and the Father is in me? The words that I speak to you I do not speak on my own. The Father who dwells in me is doing his works. Believe me that I am in the Father and the Father is in me, or else, believe because of the works themselves. Amen, amen, I say to you, whoever believes in me will do the works that I do, and will do greater ones than these, because I am going to the Father."

—John 14:6-12

Too often we can mistakenly assume that what we do, say, or offer can have little effect in the grand scheme of life. We are simply poor sinners in need of salvation, so what could we do anyway?

Jesus speaks very powerfully to what can be done by those who believe in him and follow him. "Amen, amen, I say to you, whoever believes in me will do the works that I do, and will do greater ones than these, because I am going to the Father." Greater ones than these? Think about all the miracles of Jesus recorded in sacred Scripture. You and I can do works greater than those?

St. Teresa of Avila said, "Christ has no body now on earth but yours." We are Christ to a world that needs him. It is the Christ in you that responds to the Christ in me. If it were only you alone going about doing good works and deeds, then your stewardship would amount to little.

But if you bear the name Christian, and you approach your discipleship seriously, you can truly do greater things. If you understand your stewardship as a way that Jesus works in our world, then this way of life, cultivating and sharing your gifts at every turn, becomes more valuable than all the gold in the world.

IDEA FOR RESPONSE

Do several small kind deeds for a loved one or someone you don't know. Hold the door for a stranger, make your spouse's favorite meal, bring flowers to a sick friend.

TAKE TIME TO REFLECT

What do you think is the value of your stewardship? Do you believe that through your actions — both great and small — God can touch people, heal them, and change their lives? When have you seen it happen?

ACTIONS

It's Not a Competition

"When it was evening the owner of the vineyard said to his foreman, 'Summon the laborers and give them their pay, beginning with the last and ending with the first.' When those who had started about five o'clock came, each received the usual daily wage. So when the first came, they thought that they would receive more, but each of them also got the usual wage. And on receiving it they grumbled against the landowner, saying, 'These last ones worked only one hour, and you have made them equal to us, who bore the day's burden and the heat.' He said to one of them in reply, 'My friend, I am not cheating you. Did you not agree with me for the usual daily wage? Take what is yours and go. What if I wish to give this last one the same as you? [Or] am I not free to do as I wish with my own money? Are you envious because I am generous?' Thus, the last will be first, and the first will be last."

–Matthew 20:8-16

As Everyday Stewards, I hope that each of us tries to live daily lives of generosity for the glory of God. I hope that we are all working to cultivate characteristics of a good Everyday Steward so that we can grow in maturity of faith and draw closer to Christ. But if we could accurately see on a magical computer spreadsheet how everyone else around us was living life, would it impact how we lived out our stewardship way of life? If we found out that others weren't trying as hard as we were or they were not nearly as generous, would it give us reason to pause?

In the workplace, school, and general life, people can easily look around and choose to adapt what they are doing to match more closely what others are doing. Why give work more hours if no one else is willing? Why give a 20% tip to a waiter if you suspect everyone else is only giving 15%? Why spend hours studying for a test when no one else is taking it that seriously?

Our lives of stewardship should never be measured against that of others. Even though we are all called to give all we are and all we have to God, each one of us is unique in our response to that call. Instead of any type of comparison that may temper our generosity, we should hold to the truth that the more we give of ourselves, the more fulfilled we will feel. Also, as we grow in our relationship with God, the more we will want to glorify Him. Stewardship is not a competition. It is a call to serve God without counting the cost.

IDEA FOR RESPONSE
Give a little more this week. Spend an extra 15 minutes in prayer before Mass. Tip the waitress a few more dollars. Spend 10 more minutes with a friend or family member. Can you commit to give a little more as a way of life?

TAKE TIME TO REFLECT
Name 3 experiences where you believe you worked harder than others (parish event, work, school project, etc.). Were you irritated or were you able to focus on the fact that your extra work was the right thing to do?

The Eye of a Needle

Jesus looked around and said to his disciples, "How hard it is for those who have wealth to enter the kingdom of God!" The disciples were amazed at his words. So Jesus again said to them in reply, "Children, how hard it is to enter the kingdom of God! It is easier for a camel to pass through [the] eye of [a] needle than for one who is rich to enter the kingdom of God." They were exceedingly astonished and said among themselves, "Then who can be saved?" Jesus looked at them and said, "For human beings it is impossible, but not for God. All things are possible for God."

–Mark 10:23-27

One evening at my house the skies were filled with intense lightning, and rain was pounding the windows. So the TV, along with all the other electronics, was turned off, including the lights, and the blinds were lifted so we could watch the event further unfold. My wife mentioned a family in our neighborhood that had recently lost everything in a house fire caused by a lighting strike. She asked all of us in the family, "What would you run and get if we had to leave the house due to a lightning strike?"

I mentioned that I would grab my laptop, but that was only so I could communicate with the outside world. I thought about my books, guitars, sports collectibles, clothes, electronic toys, etc. I realized that there wasn't anything I was that attached to that I felt I needed to save. Then I thought of the financial debt I had incurred because of all that stuff, and it made me wonder how that happened.

The reality is that most of us who are trying to live a stewardship way of life have been Christians much longer than good stewards. I thought I knew what being a disciple of Jesus Christ meant years ago. I had two theology degrees so I thought I already got it. Before I began taking the stewardship message to heart, I would have answered my wife's question differently.

The reality is that good stewards will see their money, time, and talent as investments in what lasts. I will need a few years to pay off my poor investment in things that were temporal and, in fact, many of them are already gone. Stewardship is a way of life that doesn't happen overnight. But when God calls us to something that requires us to leave all things behind, be sure that you own nothing that owns you.

IDEA FOR RESPONSE

Next time you are shopping at a store or online, ask yourself "Do I really need this?" before making the purchase.

TAKE TIME TO REFLECT

Name 3 possessions that perhaps "own" you more than you own them.

OWNERSHIP

Uncovering the Layers

For God so loved the world that he gave his only Son, so that everyone who believes in him might not perish but might have eternal life. For God did not send his Son into the world to condemn the world, but that the world might be saved through him. Whoever believes in him will not be condemned, but whoever does not believe has already been condemned, because he has not believed in the name of the only Son of God.

–John 3:16-18

After years working for the Church, I can honestly say that even though I feel closer to God, I still cannot fully grasp all that is God. The complexity of God has been the source of many volumes by many writers and theologians. The crazy reality of growing in a relationship with God is that the more you get to know God, the more complex God becomes.

But I think that is true of human relationships as well. I feel like I can really peg a person one way or another after only meeting him or her a few times, but my wife and children continue to perplex me. Getting to know someone means you begin to uncover the layers of personality, feeling, and emotion that make up each human being. For those who see God as only a force or a light, God is simply defined. But for those who seek to be disciples of Jesus Christ, the God we find in relationship has many layers as well.

But that which we do know for certain about God comes to us primarily from the person of Jesus. He called us to a way of life by not only teaching us about how to live, but by showing us the example of his life. Our God is defined by generosity, sacrifice, compassion, and, of course, love. The more we incorporate these characteristics into our own life, the more we bear witness to the true nature of God. Then others can see a God that is a little less complex because they understand Him through you and me. Our life will speak more than all the volumes written by all the theologians.

IDEA FOR RESPONSE

Think of someone you see often but really don't know very well. Make an effort to spend some time with him or her to get to know them better.

TAKE TIME TO REFLECT

Name 3 things you do or say that provides evidence to others of a strong relationship with God. Would others describe you as compassionate, generous, and loving?

DISCOVERY

Glimpses of Heaven

After six days Jesus took Peter, James, and John his brother, and led them up a high mountain by themselves. And he was transfigured before them; his face shone like the sun and his clothes became white as light. And behold, Moses and Elijah appeared to them, conversing with him. Then Peter said to Jesus in reply, "Lord, it is good that we are here. If you wish, I will make three tents here, one for you, one for Moses, and one for Elijah." While he was still speaking, behold, a bright cloud cast a shadow over them, then from the cloud came a voice that said, "This is my beloved Son, with whom I am well pleased; listen to him." When the disciples heard this, they fell prostrate and were very much afraid. But Jesus came and touched them, saying, "Rise, and do not be afraid." And when the disciples raised their eyes, they saw no one else but Jesus alone.

–Matthew 17:1-8

There are times in our lives when we get the chance to see a glimpse of heaven. It may be through the love of another, loved one, or stranger. Sometimes it may even be an event that seems unexplainable, perhaps even supernatural. These occurrences may be the answer to prayer, or they may surprise us by coming out of nowhere. But no matter their nature or origin, they give us hope and strength to carry on through life.

When we journey on a pathway of stewardship, we are bound to experience moments of grace where we see even the smallest seeds we planted grow into something amazing. At these moments, we are reminded that God is real and that our stewardship is not in vain. The giving of our gifts and talents is not just a response to God's calling. The giving is one way that God breaks through into the lives of others. As we use what God has given us for His glory, He uses us as instruments of grace to be truly present to others.

The greatest example of this occurs at the Mass. Through the hands of an ordained priest taking the gifts of bread and wine, God is really present with us. When we then take Christ into our bodies, we accept the offer to take him into the world to others. The world cannot see Jesus in us with human eyes, but through our works of stewardship, they can see Jesus in us. One could say they even have a chance to see a glimpse of heaven.

IDEA FOR RESPONSE
Find a quiet place and reflect on a time recently when you might say you saw a "glimpse of heaven."

TAKE TIME TO REFLECT

Name 3 times when you have witnessed God through another person or in a situation. Did you acknowledge His presence in that moment? Did you tell others about the experience?

Get Together

"This is my commandment: love one another as I love you. No one has greater love than this, to lay down one's life for one's friends. You are my friends if you do what I command you. I no longer call you slaves, because a slave does not know what his master is doing. I have called you friends, because I have told you everything I have heard from my Father. It was not you who chose me, but I who chose you and appointed you to go and bear fruit that will remain, so that whatever you ask the Father in my name he may give you. This I command you: love one another."

–John 15:12-17

A popular song in 1967 was "Get Together" by the Youngbloods. I was not alive when the song was released, but it was a song I played frequently, learning how to play guitar when I was younger. The song called for all of us to come together and "try to love one another right now." It was a song that came out in the Vietnam War era and during somewhat of a hippie revolution, but perhaps the words belong to no real moment in time. They are simply the commands of Jesus.

Sometimes we minimize the power of love by cute pop songs and slogans that mean little without action. However, we can never underestimate the power of love. Love can tear down barriers between people, change tears to laughter, and mend relationships torn apart by sin.

No option exists for disciples of Jesus Christ to not love others. Not only are we commanded to do so, but love is a gift we must pass on freely. If we give of our time, talent, and treasure, but choose not to love, we cannot claim to be truly committed disciples and good stewards. We must allow our love to bear witness to the source of all love, the Risen Jesus. This is our calling until, as the words of the Youngbloods' song states, "the one who left us here returns for us at last."

IDEA FOR RESPONSE

Take time to thank God for the people you love unconditionally and for whom love you in return.

TAKE TIME TO REFLECT

Who are the people you struggle to love ... a difficult relative, an annoying neighbor, a political leader? How can you do a better job of extending love instead of hatred?

LOVE

What Matters

Therefore, stay awake! For you do not know on which day your Lord will come. Be sure of this: if the master of the house had known the hour of night when the thief was coming, he would have stayed awake and not let his house be broken into. So too, you also must be prepared, for at an hour you do not expect, the Son of Man will come.

–Matthew 24:42-44

Over the years, my children have participated in cotillion programs. These experiences teach young people about manners, social skills, and formal dance. Some think these programs only exist for wealthy or upper-class people. I am neither one of those. I am just a parent who thinks manners still matter, that being social is a useful skill that can be learned, and that a little culture goes a long way. I can't say my children loved everything about the experience, but they did grow in appreciation of how you should treat other people. I would like to think somewhere down the road they will find themselves in a situation and will call on what they learned to succeed.

Cotillion, school, team sports, and youth ministry are all ways we prepare our kids to enter a world where Jesus Christ is seen as a foreigner, and how we live with one another is not a top concern. We teach them that they must always be ready to stand up for what's right or defend their faith or values. They must continue to cultivate those small seeds we plant in them in order to grow and bear good fruit, for their lives are gifts and the time they have been given is precious.

Good stewardship is not always about that which we can quantify or see. Who we are as people is often about that which we offer as gesture to others. It may be a kind word, a witness to the power of God, or an offer for a dance. But we must always be ready to give of ourselves graciously, for we never know when the call will come.

IDEA FOR RESPONSE

In the next few days, find a way to humble yourself and exalt others. Try letting someone take your place in line or pay extra compliments to someone.

TAKE TIME TO REFLECT

Name 3 occasions when you believe you were truly Christlike this past week. In what ways were you not?

NOTES

NOTES

NOTES

Be Mindful

The 1st Characteristic
of an Everyday Steward

Noticing the World Around Us

The next day John was there again with two of his disciples, and as he watched Jesus walk by, he said, "Behold, the Lamb of God." The two disciples heard what he said and followed Jesus. Jesus turned and saw them following him and said to them, "What are you looking for?" They said to him, "Rabbi" (which translated means Teacher), "where are you staying?" He said to them, "Come, and you will see." So they went and saw where he was staying, and they stayed with him that day. It was about four in the afternoon. Andrew, the brother of Simon Peter, was one of the two who heard John and followed Jesus. He first found his own brother Simon and told him, "We have found the Messiah" (which is translated Anointed). Then he brought him to Jesus. Jesus looked at him and said, "You are Simon the son of John; you will be called Cephas" (which is translated Peter).

–John 1:35-42

Have you ever been somewhere public and days later others said they saw you there? You can find yourself surprised that they saw you and didn't say hello. However, at least they saw you. You, on the other hand, didn't even have any idea they were around you. You may have been oblivious to what was going on, or to those crossing your path on that day. You may have been forsaking that moment thinking about another time to come down the road.

Imagine being one of those who first encountered Jesus as he began his ministry. Would you have noticed? I would like to think that I would have rushed over to him to introduce myself. But on that day when he passed on by, I just might have been caught up in life, unaware of all that was intersecting with my place in the world.

The more mindful we are of all that is around us, the more grateful we find ourselves because we take things less for granted, and the more open we are to the call of Jesus Christ. Every day, Jesus crosses our path in the form of others. They may be in need or they may have a gift to offer us. Either way, without living in the present and taking in all that God has provided for us in the day, we can miss it. I would not want to hear afterwards that Jesus saw me and I was not paying enough attention to what was around me to notice.

IDEA FOR RESPONSE

This next week, find a spot where there are several people around. Look at each person and contemplate the reality that Jesus is present in him or her.

TAKE TIME TO REFLECT

Give 3 examples of when you saw Jesus present in other people. How did they act? What did they say or do? How did they inspire you?

AWARE

The Wonders of God

"What I say to you in the darkness, speak in the light; what you hear whispered, proclaim on the housetops. And do not be afraid of those who kill the body but cannot kill the soul; rather, be afraid of the one who can destroy both soul and body in Gehenna. Are not two sparrows sold for a small coin? Yet not one of them falls to the ground without your Father's knowledge. Even all the hairs of your head are counted. So do not be afraid; you are worth more than many sparrows."

–Matthew 10:27-31

When I was a teenager, after a homecoming dance one year I took my date for a walk on the Potomac in downtown Alexandria. The moon was out, and I was struck by how the light shimmered on the water. I remember focusing to try to see all the details of the dancing rays on the ripples. My date didn't see it and didn't really get it. She thought it was no big deal. It was a great date and a fun night, but for that one moment, we saw the world from two completely different vantage points.

Two of the greatest gifts from God to each of us are life and time. Without taking care, we can easily miss the grandeur and beauty of both. Being mindful as an Everyday Steward means pausing to see the detail in all that exists around us. God's creation is not something created with a broad brush, but instead with the intricacies of a master painter.

God created all things with purpose and a complexity that only the divine could fully comprehend. Every single hair on our head has been counted! But when we take a moment to reflect on the beauty that is created by that complexity, we allow ourselves to revel in God's generosity. There is so much to give thanks for in this life. But you and I can't give thanks to God unless we really stop to take notice.

IDEA FOR RESPONSE

On a clear night this week, head outdoors to look at the moon and stars, praising God for all His wonders.

TAKE TIME TO REFLECT

Name 3 times when you were awestruck by the beauty of nature. Did others share the experiences with you? If you were alone, did you tell others about the experiences and how you saw God?

CREATION

Owe Only Love

Owe nothing to anyone, except to love one another; for the one who loves another has fulfilled the law. The commandments, "You shall not commit adultery; you shall not kill; you shall not steal; you shall not covet," and whatever other commandment there may be, are summed up in this saying, namely "You shall love your neighbor as yourself." Love does no evil to the neighbor; hence, love is the fulfillment of the law.

–Romans 13:8-10

I have to smile when I read in St. Paul's Letter to the Romans, "Owe nothing to anyone, except to love one another." I smile because I know that in today's world, few people owe nothing to anyone. We have credit card debt, mortgages, student loans, car loans, and new loans to consolidate old loans. It would seem that we actually owe everything to everyone.

These debts are of this world. I am pretty sure no one residing in heaven is still making mortgage payments. We have created contracts in this world to make possible certain transactions of goods, services, and shelter. But there is one thing that we naturally owe one another and that lasts longer than our time on earth: love.

You do not need to take out a loan to have more love to give. There also is no limit to the love you have been given to share. However, it is the one gift that we sometimes treat with the least respect. We hold back love due to sins of pride, prejudice, and apathy. We distort and manipulate love for our own gain and selfish desires. We can find ourselves placing more importance on the things for which we have taken out loans than the love that is eternal.

I am trying the best I can to get to a point where I no longer owe anything to banks and mortgage lenders. I don't want to leave this world owing anyone for the earthly things I had in this life. But even more importantly, I realize the shame it would be to leave people behind who didn't get enough love from me. There is nothing greater than love.

IDEA FOR RESPONSE

Call (don't email or text!) a family member you don't see very often and tell them how much you love them.

TAKE TIME TO REFLECT

When have you withheld love from someone because you were afraid of getting hurt? Who receives your unconditional love?

ETERNAL

Buried in Your Backyard

"It will be as when a man who was going on a journey called in his servants and entrusted his possessions to them. To one he gave five talents; to another, two; to a third, one—to each according to his ability. Then he went away. Immediately the one who received five talents went and traded with them, and made another five. Likewise, the one who received two made another two. But the man who received one went off and dug a hole in the ground and buried his master's money."

–Matthew 25:14-18

I remember watching a television show about a high school that dug up a time capsule that students had buried 25 years earlier. They had buried it with the purpose of showing others many years later the trends of the day and how student life was at that time. It was a fun exercise and everyone — the current students as well as those now grown — laughed at the clothing styles, corny photos, and lack of technology from years ago.

I wonder how the former students felt about how they had grown in those 25 years. How many of them realized their high school dreams? Did they find their purpose in this world and feel fulfilled in life? Did they use the talents and gifts God gave them to really make a difference in the world?

We have all been given talents and gifts by God to be cultivated and offered back to Him and those around us for His glory. As time has passed, hopefully we have taken seriously our stewardship of these gifts. But sometimes out of fear, misunderstanding, or even apathy, we have taken one or more of our gifts and buried them, hiding them away from others and stifling all growth. This is no way to honor God and certainly not a path to fulfillment in life. If we have anything buried in our backyard, we might do well to dig it back up, clean it up, and begin building upon it. Like a time capsule, those things will not be buried forever. One day the giver of that gift will ask what you have done with it. When that day comes, I pray you don't need to find a shovel.

IDEA FOR RESPONSE

Go through an old box of your photos, letters, and memorabilia. Reflect on what used to be important to you and what's important now.

TAKE TIME TO REFLECT

Name 3 gifts or talents you need to cultivate and share more. Why, at times, have you buried these in the first place?

GROWTH

The Face of Christ

"He will place the sheep on his right and the goats on his left. Then the king will say to those on his right, 'Come, you who are blessed by my Father. Inherit the kingdom prepared for you from the foundation of the world. For I was hungry and you gave me food, I was thirsty and you gave me drink, a stranger and you welcomed me, naked and you clothed me, ill and you cared for me, in prison and you visited me.' Then the righteous will answer him and say, 'Lord, when did we see you hungry and feed you, or thirsty and give you drink? When did we see you a stranger and welcome you, or naked and clothe you? When did we see you ill or in prison, and visit you?' And the king will say to them in reply, 'Amen, I say to you, whatever you did for one of these least brothers of mine, you did for me.'"

–Matthew 25:33-40

One day when I was walking the city streets where I was giving a series of talks, I saw what appeared to be an older woman hunched over with a sign asking for help. At first I passed her on my way to visit the local drugstore. But then I came back around when I realized that I had not been very mindful upon first seeing her. I didn't have much cash to give her, but as I always tell everyone else in my talks, oftentimes what people need more than cash is someone to at least acknowledge them. I reached into my pocket to give her what little I had, and I simply said, "Hello. I hope you are okay and I hope you can use this."

When her face turned toward me, I saw she was probably only about 16 years of age and she was very beautiful. She smiled immediately and said how much this meant to her. She gathered up her few belongings, and I watched her walk to a café for a meal. I turned to walk back to my lodging and I thought to myself, "She could have been my daughter." That's when the still, small voice spoke to me saying, "Don't you understand? That *was* your daughter!"

A young homeless girl on the street can take on so many forms: stranger, neighbor, daughter, and Jesus. Unless we are mindful of those in our midst, we miss the chance to see any of them. We must never be fooled by appearance. That day I almost missed seeing my Lord.

IDEA FOR RESPONSE
The next time you see someone on the street begging for food or money, give them something without fear, judgment, or skepticism.

TAKE TIME TO REFLECT

Name 3 ways in which you help God's sons or daughters in need. When have you turned your back to them?

Use Your Gifts Wisely

Jesus said, "To what shall we compare the kingdom of God, or what parable can we use for it? It is like a mustard seed that, when it is sown in the ground, is the smallest of all the seeds on the earth. But once it is sown, it springs up and becomes the largest of plants and puts forth large branches, so that the birds of the sky can dwell in its shade."

–Mark 4:30-32

You could buy a meal for a person who is hungry or for a person who just ate a feast. You could spend time with a lonely person or with someone who has more friends than you. You could step forward to join a parish committee that your experience and knowledge can help, or you can join a ministry where you will constantly struggle to figure out what to do. All of the above actions involve you giving and sharing yourself and your gifts. But not all of these actions will bear good fruit.

If a sower sows seeds only on rocky or weed-infested soil, nothing of great value will grow. But if that same sower plants his seeds in rich soil, then the harvest will one day be great. In all of the soils, the seed is being sown, but it is not the act of sowing that is the most important factor.

In living a stewardship way of life, we must discern how best to share our gifts. Discernment needs the Holy Spirit and a desire to follow God's will, not our own. Our own desires and misconceptions can cause us to use our gifts unwisely. The more mindful we are of how, when, and why we are sharing ourselves, than the greater the impact for God's glory. God wants all of you, but not in a way that is without understanding and discernment. He wants you to shine as a light to the world through your stewardship just as He came to you as the Light of the World in Baptism. You can't shine brightly if the match does not hit the wick.

IDEA FOR RESPONSE

Spend 15 minutes in prayer asking God to grant you the gift of discernment.

TAKE TIME TO REFLECT

Think of a position you held (either as an employee or volunteer) where it was not a great fit for your natural talents. Were you satisfied in that role? Did you turn to the Holy Spirit for guidance?

Turn Away from Temptation

Jesus was led by the Spirit into the desert to be tempted by the devil. He fasted for forty days and forty nights, and afterwards he was hungry. The tempter approached and said to him, "If you are the Son of God, command that these stones become loaves of bread." He said in reply, "It is written:
> *'One does not live by bread alone,*
> *but by every word that comes forth from the mouth of God.'"*

–Matthew 4:1-4

We can look at the lives of teenagers in today's world and sometimes wonder how they can ever survive. Due to technology and the constant drone of mass media, young people are under constant attack by forces that are anything but Christian. Of course, if we are honest, it isn't just the young that are susceptible to these temptations, for any age can be caught off guard and fall into a trap where he or she then wonders, "Why did I do that?" You can imagine then how someone with less maturity and life experience can easily be deceived by the culture.

Jesus was fully human and fully divine. The humanity in him certainly understood the allure of temptation. While he was in the desert, Satan tried all he could to shake Jesus from his principles. But at no time did Jesus lose his composure and give in to temptation. He was constantly mindful of his surroundings, his adversary, and who he was and who he was not.

When we are ever aware of the forces surrounding us, both good and bad, and when we are constantly listening and looking for God interacting with us, we are able to respond to God's call in daily life. We can also see evil for its true self and not be taken in by it. Whether we are young or old, to be aware of and living in the present, without the baggage of the past and without fear of the future, will allow us to stay true to ourselves and to Jesus. We will be able to give of ourselves freely without concern for what the culture might say. That is good news.

IDEA FOR RESPONSE

Receive the Sacrament of Reconciliation and ask God to forgive your sinful thoughts and actions.

TAKE TIME TO REFLECT

Name 3 times when you were tempted to turn toward sin and away from God. Did you give in or did you hold true to your principles?

RESIST

Building the Foundation

He told them a parable. "There was a rich man whose land produced a bountiful harvest. He asked himself, 'What shall I do, for I do not have space to store my harvest?' And he said, 'This is what I shall do: I shall tear down my barns and build larger ones. There I shall store all my grain and other goods and I shall say to myself, "Now as for you, you have so many good things stored up for many years, rest, eat, drink, be merry!"' But God said to him, 'You fool, this night your life will be demanded of you; and the things you have prepared, to whom will they belong?'"

–Luke 12:16-20

In the Church, we like to build things. We build churches, parish centers, schools, and many more brick-and-mortar structures to carry on with our mission. We also build things that are not as tangible. We build engagement. We try to increase the offertory. We work to increase the number of people in programs. We try to fill more seats on a Sunday. Hopefully, we do all these things to help fulfill our mission, which is to bring people to Jesus Christ and assist them in becoming mature and intentional disciples. But having spent over 20 years in parish ministry, I realize that is not always the case.

As individuals, we can fall prey to the same temptations as a parish community. We begin to lose sight of why we live a stewardship way of life and why we were called in our Baptism to share with others the good news. We compete with others, much like a parish sometimes competes with the parish across town. We may find ourselves doing things without thought or reflection, performing these tasks simply because that is what we have always done. Finally, we may limit our role in God's plan because we fear not having the time, talent, or money to accomplish what God has asked of us. We become more practical and less trusting in God's promises.

The reality is that there will come a day when all our churches, parish centers, and schools will be no more. All we have stored up as communities and individuals will cease to exist. All that will remain is God and those who love Him. We can never lose sight of why we do what we do: eternal life with

Jesus Christ. Will there be a list at the end of your life of all those you helped lead to the Father? I do not know. But if there is one, my prayer for each of us is that it is very, very long.

IDEA FOR RESPONSE
Look up the Baptismal Promises online. Say them out loud and recommit yourself to living a Christlike life.

TAKE TIME TO REFLECT

What emotions would you feel if the church where you worshipped would tragically burn to the ground? Would you lose hope or would your faith remain strong? How could you remain strong for the other parishioners?

EVANGELIZE

Facebook Fans of Jesus

Someone asked him, "Lord, will only a few people be saved?" He answered them, "Strive to enter through the narrow door, for many, I tell you, will attempt to enter but will not be strong enough. After the master of the house has arisen and locked the door, then will you stand outside knocking and saying, 'Lord, open the door for us.' He will say to you in reply, 'I do not know where you are from.' And you will say, 'We ate and drank in your company and you taught in our streets.' Then he will say to you, 'I do not know where you are from. Depart from me, all you evildoers!'"

–Luke 13:23-27

Facebook, Twitter, and other forms of social media can be powerful tools of communication. They allow people to stay in touch. They provide an avenue for fresh ideas. People can be engaged in conversations and be exposed to issues of the day in ways few could have dreamed of just a few decades ago. But social media can also give the false sense of really knowing someone, when only the surface has been scratched about who a person is in reality.

You don't really know someone just because you know a lot about him or her and are linked to a profile online. Unfortunately, people develop emotional attachments to the idea of a person all the time. If they do find themselves fortunate enough to meet the person face-to-face one day, they can often find out they never really knew the person in the first place.

There are people who believe they know Jesus so very well. They can readily share their view of what Jesus would do or wouldn't do in a given situation. They own items like crosses and Bibles that seem to provide evidence of this person they know so well. Sometimes, they even strongly admonish others because their view of Jesus is certainly not in line with their own.

But Jesus speaks about those who claim to know him, but they really do not belong to him at all. They make claims based upon what they have seen and heard, but they have never allowed Jesus to truly change them. They are like Facebook followers, seemingly close but with no real relationship at all.

IDEA FOR RESPONSE
Reach out to a friend on social media and ask them to meet for coffee so you can chat face to face.

TAKE TIME TO REFLECT

Do you really know Jesus? How can you invite him into your life and let a real relationship develop?

What Are You Here for Anyway?

I am speaking as to sensible people; judge for yourselves what I am saying. The cup of blessing that we bless, is it not a participation in the blood of Christ? The bread that we break, is it not a participation in the body of Christ? Because the loaf of bread is one, we, though many, are one body, for we all partake of the one loaf.

–1 Corinthians 10:15-17

When I was younger, for many years I helped lead the music for our parish liturgies. The "grander" liturgies stand out to me: first Communion, Confirmation, Christmas, etc. It was at one of those first Communion Masses where I learned an important lesson.

As musicians at liturgy, you really play a key role in providing a sense of movement to the entire experience. Between moments of spoken prayer and petition, you provide a way for all assembled to pray with song. Sometimes, you make decisions at the moment for the sake of keeping the liturgy "moving."

When it was time for Communion, we played throughout the entire time, and I did not allow a time for us as musicians to receive ourselves. I had hoped that this would be noticed, and after our playing had concluded, someone would offer us the Eucharist. They didn't. At first I thought, "Unfortunately, that's just the way it goes." One of our musicians did not see it that way and was upset. He said to me, "What am I here for, anyway?"

My assumption without thinking much about it that day was that our presence was to lead music. However, I had missed it. Even though we played an important role at the liturgy, the reason we were there was Jesus. No matter how beautiful our music could be or how well the congregation sang, our primary purpose of being there was just like everyone else's: Jesus.

Our stewardship is very important, but at no time does it become the main thing. Our generosity and commitment of ourselves point to that which matters the most. When we lose sight of why we are doing something and whom we are doing it for, our actions can become hollow. The music of our efforts offers praise to the One who makes that melody even possible in the first place.

IDEA FOR RESPONSE
Do a spiritual examination at the end of each day, reflecting on whether your thoughts, attitudes, behaviors, and actions were in the manner of Christ.

TAKE TIME TO REFLECT

Name 3 times when you had been so focused on doing good deeds that you overlooked the point of doing the good deed in the first place. How can you be more mindful of your purpose?

PURPOSE

NOTES

NOTES

NOTES

Be Prayerful

The 2nd Characteristic
of an Everyday Steward

Looking for a Star

Herod called the magi secretly and ascertained from them the time of the star's appearance. He sent them to Bethlehem and said, "Go and search diligently for the child. When you have found him, bring me word, that I too may go and do him homage." After their audience with the king they set out. And behold, the star that they had seen at its rising preceded them, until it came and stopped over the place where the child was. They were overjoyed at seeing the star, and on entering the house they saw the child with Mary his mother. They prostrated themselves and did him homage. Then they opened their treasures and offered him gifts of gold, frankincense, and myrrh. And having been warned in a dream not to return to Herod, they departed for their country by another way.

–Matthew 2:7-12

The story of the Wise Men bringing gifts to Jesus, the newborn King, is a great one, isn't it? They had a great big star in the sky to lead the way. I am no Boy Scout, so I am not sure how well I would do following a star like that. But the important point here is that God led them to the manger. The manger was a place where, unless God specifically showed you this was where the Christ Child was born, you wouldn't have believed it. You would have passed on by.

In our lives, there are no big stars in the sky leading us where we need to go. It isn't so easy sometimes discerning where God is leading us. We may seek to use our gifts wisely, but in what manner and to what end is not always clear.

This is where prayer can make a huge difference. If we seek to cultivate a prayer life where we are mindful of the presence of God throughout our day, then the call is easier to discern. We can help the process by intentionally offering to God in the morning the entirety of the day to come: all our actions, all our time, and all our decisions. In the evening, we can examine the past hours of the day and reflect on when we responded well to Christ's call and when we fell short. Then we resolve to begin again tomorrow, inviting Christ to be with us every step of the way. God may not offer a star in the sky to lead us, but if we invite Him on our journey each day, the path will be much clearer.

IDEA FOR RESPONSE

Print off a finger labyrinth. Slowly trace the pattern of the labyrinth, clearing your mind of thoughts and focusing on following the path. When you reach the center, take a moment to reflect on the guidance you need from God. Retrace your path out of the labyrinth.

TAKE TIME TO REFLECT

Give 3 examples of how prayer guided you through a difficult decision in your life. What did you ask of God? Where did He lead you?

GUIDANCE

Recognizing the Voice of Jesus

So Jesus said again, "Amen, amen, I say to you, I am the gate for the sheep. All who came [before me] are thieves and robbers, but the sheep did not listen to them. I am the gate. Whoever enters through me will be saved, and will come in and go out and find pasture. A thief comes only to steal and slaughter and destroy; I came so that they might have life and have it more abundantly. I am the good shepherd. A good shepherd lays down his life for the sheep. A hired man, who is not a shepherd and whose sheep are not his own, sees a wolf coming and leaves the sheep and runs away, and the wolf catches and scatters them. This is because he works for pay and has no concern for the sheep. I am the good shepherd, and I know mine and mine know me, just as the Father knows me and I know the Father; and I will lay down my life for the sheep."

–John 10:7-15

When my wireless provider introduced HD Voice, the voice I heard on my phone was unbelievably clear, and it felt at times like both the caller and I were in the same room. The best aspect of this feature is that it didn't cost the customer any additional fees, and it didn't require any changes to the phone. I could say it was free, but I suspect I was already paying for it in my monthly bill anyway. At least it felt free.

The clearer the voice calling you, the easier it is to recognize who it is on the other end of the call. In John's Gospel, Jesus speaks of the gatekeeper who opens the gate and calls for his sheep. They respond because they know his voice. Others try to lure the sheep when the gatekeeper is not there, but the sheep find their voices unclear or unfamiliar.

Jesus is our gatekeeper. But unlike receiving something for free from a wireless company, to be able to hear his voice we need to pay attention and practice listening. By developing a stewardship way of life that is mindful and prayerful, we become attuned to his voice and are able to discern when the call is from our Lord and when it is from an imposter. It is great to talk about all the things we can do and all the gifts we can share, but if are not listening for his call to hear where our offerings are needed, we can end up like a lost sheep searching for the gatekeeper.

IDEA FOR RESPONSE

When you sit down for daily prayer, flip to any page in the Bible and randomly point to a verse. Read it and listen to hear how God is talking to you through it.

TAKE TIME TO REFLECT

Write about a time when God was calling you. What was He asking you to do? Did you listen to what He was saying or did you turn away?

To Be with God

When Jesus had said this, he raised his eyes to heaven and said, "Father, the hour has come. Give glory to your son, so that your son may glorify you, just as you gave him authority over all people, so that he may give eternal life to all you gave him. Now this is eternal life, that they should know you, the only true God, and the one whom you sent, Jesus Christ. I glorified you on earth by accomplishing the work that you gave me to do. Now glorify me, Father, with you, with the glory that I had with you before the world began."

–John 17:1-5

I don't think I am giving away anything to say that Knights of Columbus are supposed to always carry with them a rosary. Even before I became a Knight, often I would carry a rosary with me. Like most good habits, at times I would slowly become oblivious and forget to have it with me. Many weeks and months of carrying it in my pocket would give way to a couple weeks of wondering where it went. To stick with any practice, you have to be intentional and mindful of what you are doing.

A good prayer life requires commitment. Carrying a rosary isn't really prayer because the prayers are not being said. However, a rosary or other religious article does serve as a reminder of who we are and to whom we belong. A prayer life should not be one where we simply seek to recite words, but one where we walk in the presence of God at all times. Prayer is about presence.

An Everyday Steward will find success in cultivating a prayer life by inviting God into all aspects and moments of the day. Recited prayer throughout the day serves as the formal ritual part of our relationship with God. In all relationships, we have standard things we say to each other about love, our needs, and our hopes for that person. It is what takes place between the words that sometimes makes the difference.

IDEA FOR RESPONSE

Find time to say the rosary at least 3 times this week. Carry one in your pocket and let it remind you of the presence of Christ in your daily living.

TAKE TIME TO REFLECT

When do you pray? Is it only at certain times of the day? Name 3 ways in which you can incorporate prayer into more moments of your life.

PRESENCE

Sowing Good Seed

Jesus spoke to them at length in parables, saying: "A sower went out to sow. And as he sowed, some seed fell on the path, and birds came and ate it up. Some fell on rocky ground, where it had little soil. It sprang up at once because the soil was not deep, and when the sun rose it was scorched, and it withered for lack of roots. Some seed fell among thorns, and the thorns grew up and choked it. But some seed fell on rich soil, and produced fruit, a hundred or sixty or thirtyfold."

–Matthew 13:3-8

Over the years, I have wasted a lot: a lot of money, a lot of time, and a lot of talent. Sometimes I didn't realize I was wasting these things, but after reflection, I realized I could have done more and accomplished much greater things. Of course, I think that is part of our imperfect humanity. It truly is easier for us to waste our gifts than grow them into something more.

The parable of the sower speaks about the word of God that gets planted in our hearts. If the soil of our heart is rich, than the word will grow and change us. If that soil is rocky or full of weeds, the word will lie there without any impact, bearing no fruit.

This parable can be applied to living a stewardship way of life as well. As sowers, we have been given the seeds of our time, talent, and treasure. We have a choice of where to plant these gifts. As good Everyday Stewards, we are called to plant them wisely and prudently. Oftentimes it is not enough to simply give away what we have. We need to discern the best places to sow these gifts so the maximum harvest can grow. This takes prayer, reflection, and study. Without a solid discernment process, we can find ourselves sowing seeds endlessly without much to show for it. But joyful is the person who has used one's gifts wisely, for the bounty of the harvest is great.

IDEA FOR RESPONSE

Reread the parable of the sower, imagining yourself as the sower. Pray then for God's help in better discerning your future acts of giving.

TAKE TIME TO REFLECT

What is your discernment process when a difficult decision needs to be made? How can you apply that process when asking God for direction on using your time, talent, and treasure?

WISDOM

God's GPS Never Fails

As he passed by the Sea of Galilee, he saw Simon and his brother Andrew casting their nets into the sea; they were fishermen. Jesus said to them, "Come after me, and I will make you fishers of men." Then they abandoned their nets and followed him. He walked along a little farther and saw James, the son of Zebedee, and his brother John. They too were in a boat mending their nets. Then he called them. So they left their father Zebedee in the boat along with the hired men and followed him.

–Mark 1:16-20

I use GPS wherever I go, and it serves me well most of the time. However, sometimes it leads me to a place that does not exist. Then there are those times when I am about to turn, and the man inside my phone shouts out, "GPS signal lost!" or "Rerouting!" The problem is when the area is unfamiliar to me, I have no choice but to listen. I could try to get where I am going by simple intuition or by pulling over to look at a paper map, but I don't trust my sense of direction and haven't bought a paper map in close to a decade.

Many people move through life without any direction. They find themselves constantly rerouting and wondering when they will ever get to a satisfying final destination. What they need is a compass and a companion for the journey, yet they have no idea how to get either.

Prayer can serve as a compass, and it connects us to a companion for the journey. Stewardship living is impossible without prayer. If we count on our own will and believe we can become fruitful without daily contact with the divine, we can find ourselves looking for directions more than moving toward a destination. God, through prayer, will help us see all we have as a gift. God, through prayer, will lead us away from materialism and selfishness, and toward freedom and generosity. Even when we fall to sin, the path back is clearer. God's GPS signal is never really lost.

IDEA FOR RESPONSE

Begin each day this week asking God to lead you to opportunities for great generosity.

TAKE TIME TO REFLECT

Reflect on a time in your life when you didn't follow your moral compass and you lost sight of your faith. How did you get back on course and reconnect with God? Do you find yourself lost now?

COMPASS

I Can See Clearly Now

On hearing that it was Jesus of Nazareth, he began to cry out and say, "Jesus, son of David, have pity on me." And many rebuked him, telling him to be silent. But he kept calling out all the more, "Son of David, have pity on me." Jesus stopped and said, "Call him." So they called the blind man, saying to him, "Take courage; get up, he is calling you." He threw aside his cloak, sprang up, and came to Jesus. Jesus said to him in reply, "What do you want me to do for you?" The blind man replied to him, "Master, I want to see." Jesus told him, "Go your way; your faith has saved you." Immediately he received his sight and followed him on the way.

–Mark 10:47-52

Yes, I am getting older. I am reminded every time I try to sing at Mass, cook a meal, take medication, assemble a newly purchased product, or even read my child's report card. I cannot see! I used to get so frustrated and even feel helpless. Now I have reading glasses everywhere. I used to have one pair, but that was ridiculous. I never had them when I needed them. So now I have them everywhere: each room of my house, each vehicle, etc. If I find myself in a situation where I cannot see and I have no glasses nearby, I have only myself to blame.

We can often be blinded in situations that call for a response of stewardship. We find ourselves oblivious to the needs of others. We miss the signals that we are being called to give of ourselves to a cause, a community, or an individual. The seemingly important things in life block our vision to the smaller everyday callings that Jesus places in our path.

The main reason why this occurs is that we fail to avail ourselves of the help that Jesus offers. Do we really think that we can be good stewards all on our own? I think of the words of Psalm 119 (or more truthfully the words of an old Amy Grant song), "Thy word is a lamp unto my feet, and a light unto my path."

Just like the blind man, without Jesus Christ, we can't really see a thing. Some of life is obvious, but most of life is far from it. When we look at things through the lens that Jesus provides, stewardship opportunities are everywhere. Jesus provides this lens when we dedicate ourselves to prayer, study, and virtue. The good news is you can then take the lens wherever you go. If you find yourself in a situation where you cannot see, you have only yourself to blame.

IDEA FOR RESPONSE
Ask God to help you be a good steward by reading Psalm 119:105-112.

TAKE TIME TO REFLECT

Recall a time when you could not find the answer to some dilemma until you turned to God. Why didn't you turn to Him first?

SIGHT

The Extraordinary as Ordinary

While he was praying his face changed in appearance and his clothing became dazzling white. And behold, two men were conversing with him, Moses and Elijah, who appeared in glory and spoke of his exodus that he was going to accomplish in Jerusalem. Peter and his companions had been overcome by sleep, but becoming fully awake, they saw his glory and the two men standing with him. As they were about to part from him, Peter said to Jesus, "Master, it is good that we are here; let us make three tents, one for you, one for Moses, and one for Elijah." But he did not know what he was saying.

–Luke 9:29-33

I remember when I was younger, being on a retreat and praying alone in a chapel for the successful talk a friend was giving at the same time. What was different on this day was I decided to pray the psalms aloud since no one else was there to judge either my singing ability or my mode of prayer. For about 30 minutes I sang aloud, one psalm after another. Towards the end of my prayer time, I felt a very strong presence of God. There is much more to the story, but suffice to say that it was an experience that made me break down into tears and one that I will never forget. God had broken through my ordinary life and was present to me in a way that was extraordinary.

I often tell people that one reason I love being Catholic is that, for us, the supernatural is really the natural. We believe bread and wine become Jesus Christ, we understand the supernatural reality of all the sacraments, and we hopefully are never surprised when we see the powerful results of prayer. There should be no separation between our ordinary lives in the natural world and the elements of the supernatural world.

When the Apostles see Moses and Elijah before them in this week's Gospel from Luke, they want to immediately pitch tents for them to stay. That is a pretty natural response to the supernatural. What would your response be to seeing Moses and Elijah? Fear? Confusion? Hospitality?

The goal is to make our entire day a prayer and to allow God into every moment. The more we practice this type of prayer, the more the supernatural and the natural blend. We become more open to being used by God for His glory. And who knows, the chance may increase that one day we might just say without surprise, "Hello, Moses and Elijah! Would you like something to drink?"

IDEA FOR RESPONSE
Try to add a new way of praying to your usual routine. Are you one to recite prayers? Try singing some psalms. Are you more of a free-form prayer? Say the rosary.

TAKE TIME TO REFLECT

Have you ever had an experience where you were overwhelmed by the presence of God while praying? Write about it.

The Generosity of God

"And I tell you, ask and you will receive; seek and you will find; knock and the door will be opened to you. For everyone who asks, receives; and the one who seeks, finds; and to the one who knocks, the door will be opened. What father among you would hand his son a snake when he asks for a fish? Or hand him a scorpion when he asks for an egg? If you then, who are wicked, know how to give good gifts to your children, how much more will the Father in heaven give the holy Spirit to those who ask him?"

–Luke 11:9-13

My father would always say to me when I was growing up, "Whatever is mine is yours." He was always very generous toward me and, if I am being truthful, probably spoiled me. We were not a rich family by any measure, but I never really wanted for anything. If I asked, I would receive.

Jesus tells us our heavenly Father is similar to my father, but God is profoundly more generous. However, I am not sure many of us really believe that. When growing up, we ask our earthly parents for all sorts of things, some requests being large but many being small. I know my own three children might ask me for anything at anytime. If God is more generous with me than I am with my own three children, how come I find myself mostly asking God for things when all my other options have run out, or my back is against the wall? We make deals with God in our moment of despair or fear, but when things are great, we ask for little or sometimes nothing at all.

We need God and His generosity 365 days a year. Better than that, God wants us to ask for things and to learn to rely on Him. There is no strength in walking in this world alone. God wants to be the source of all our strength. That is one reason why at every hour of the day, somewhere in the world, Mass is being celebrated and His children are receiving Him in the holy Eucharist.

If God can become man, die, and rise again, and then humble Himself in the elements of bread and wine to be close to you, do you not think

He will respond to your everyday simple requests? May God's generosity flow to you in great abundance, for His love knows no limits.

IDEA FOR RESPONSE

Make note of the prayer requests you've received this week and include them in your daily prayers.

TAKE TIME TO REFLECT

Name 3 times when you made deals with God in prayer. What were the deals you proposed? Did you keep your end of the bargain in each instance?

ASK

See with the Eyes of Jesus

"There was a rich man who dressed in purple garments and fine linen and dined sumptuously each day. And lying at his door was a poor man named Lazarus, covered with sores, who would gladly have eaten his fill of the scraps that fell from the rich man's table. Dogs even used to come and lick his sores. When the poor man died, he was carried away by angels to the bosom of Abraham. The rich man also died and was buried, and from the netherworld, where he was in torment, he raised his eyes and saw Abraham far off and Lazarus at his side."

–Luke 16:19-23

I would like to think that most people in the world would help someone who was suffering if they had the chance. I guess my optimism starts to take a hit when I consider that in some cases, the cost will be higher for that help than in others. To help someone with a meal or to transport someone to a doctor is one thing. To offer oneself completely, all of one's money or time, is quite another.

Of course, there have been famous examples of this type of giving. St. Teresa of Calcutta comes to mind. But I personally know of others who have given everything for another. Friends who have adopted an older child, gone to live as missionaries in a far-off land, or added on to their house in order to care for an aging parent, are all examples to me of those who answer the call without counting the cost.

I am not concerned with not being able to follow the examples of these stewardship heroes. What concerns me is becoming too comfortable and not noticing the Lazarus that may be in my midst. Living a life of Everyday Stewardship means not only answering the call when it is obvious and when we have the chance to truly do something amazing, but also when it is less obvious and the need not as easily noticeable. Who doesn't want to help the starving child they see on a late night infomercial? But the sad reality is that sometimes there are children lying at our proverbial door that fail to gain our attention.

So, I pray to see with the eyes of Jesus. I ask that I may be ever more mindful of those in need who cross my path. I pray to see Jesus in them. I pray to be Jesus to them. I pray that I may answer the call.

IDEA FOR RESPONSE
This week, consider visiting an elderly relative or neighbor who is homebound.

TAKE TIME TO REFLECT

Do you always notice the people at your feet who are in need?
How can you do better at seeing with the eyes of Jesus?

ATTENTION

Love God Enthusiastically

Now a man there named Zacchaeus, who was a chief tax collector and also a wealthy man, was seeking to see who Jesus was; but he could not see him because of the crowd, for he was short in stature. So he ran ahead and climbed a sycamore tree in order to see Jesus, who was about to pass that way. When he reached the place, Jesus looked up and said to him, "Zacchaeus, come down quickly, for today I must stay at your house." And he came down quickly and received him with joy.

–Luke 19:2-6

My wife is on the shorter side so she has always had a great love for the story of Zacchaeus, the wealthy tax collector who was too small to see Jesus over the crowd so he climbed a tree in order to see better. For many years, she was a catechist and loved telling that story to children because by their age alone they were short. My wife and Zacchaeus are proof that good things come in small packages. But Zacchaeus' size is not why Jesus showed him favor. It was his faith in Jesus and his eagerness to serve him.

Climbing a tree is not always a safe way to gain a better vantage point to see. But if you were really moved to see someone very important, you might risk it. Hosting someone in your house who you admire or want desperately to please can be nerve-racking. But the chance to be near that person and show your love makes it all worth it. And it is not an easy commitment to change one's entire life and become a new person. But if you believed that the one asking you was the source of all life, the commitment might be seen as a necessity.

We should pray every day for the desire and excitement of Zacchaeus when it comes to our relationship with Jesus Christ. If we are intentional disciples, we have had an encounter with the Lord much like Zacchaeus. However, our decision to live a stewardship way of life can sometimes be delayed. If we are like Zacchaeus, our sheer love of Christ will propel us to give all we have to him and resolve to live transformed lives of generosity. No matter how small we are, it is the enormity of our love for God and His love for us that makes all the difference.

IDEA FOR RESPONSE
Find 15 minutes to listen to some upbeat Christian or faith-filled music and let the Holy Spirit wash over you.

TAKE TIME TO REFLECT

Have you ever been really excited to see a well-known person, maybe a singer, author, or politician? If you had been alive during Jesus' time, what lengths would you have gone to see him, to touch him?

ENTHUSIASM

NOTES

NOTES

NOTES

Be Grateful

*The 3rd Characteristic
of an Everyday Steward*

Simple Things

Job spoke, saying:
Is not life on earth a drudgery,
  its days like those of a hireling?
Like a slave who longs for the shade,
  a hireling who waits for wages,
So I have been assigned months of futility,
  and troubled nights have been counted off for me.

–Job 7:1-3

Sometimes we can feel like we are living the life of Job: everything is going wrong all at the same time. Everyone finds himself or herself in a valley once in awhile. How we got there is not nearly as important as how are we going to get out.

Everyday Stewards are called to be grateful for all things, large and small. It is easier to be grateful for obvious things like family, health, and life itself, than it is to look for the ordinary gifts in our life. When we cultivate a sense of wonder and thankfulness for the many little things in life, we find ourselves more resilient in times of trial. We can look out our window and see all those gifts in creation. We can look around our home and see all the things people take too easily for granted.

Imagine life without some of the simplest things, like clothing, warmth, water, and furniture. There are people in this world who long for all of those things. But God has given them for your benefit and for you to share with others.

IDEA FOR RESPONSE

Create a list of at least 10 things you normally take for granted and add to it from time to time. When life seems hard, bring out the list and let gratefulness lift you up and out of your plight so that once again you can be about your Father's work.

TAKE TIME TO REFLECT

Name 3 times in your life when nothing seemed to be going right. Was there anything you did to get through the situation? Did you appreciate the simple things?

Appreciate Your Family

I give thanks to my God always on your account for the grace of God bestowed on you in Christ Jesus, that in him you were enriched in every way, with all discourse and all knowledge, as the testimony to Christ was confirmed among you, so that you are not lacking in any spiritual gift as you wait for the revelation of our Lord Jesus [Christ]. He will keep you firm to the end, irreproachable on the day of our Lord Jesus Christ. God is faithful, and by him you were called to fellowship with his Son, Jesus Christ our Lord.

–1 Corinthians 1:4-9

Pope Francis once said in a homily, "If families can say these three things, they will be fine. 'Sorry,' 'Excuse me,' and 'Thank you.' How often do we say 'Thank you' in our families? How often do we say 'Thank you' to those who help us, those close to us, those at our side throughout life? All too often we take everything for granted!" (Homily, October 13, 2013).

The reason we fail to thank our loved ones is not that we are without thanks. It is that we get into routines and become numbed by the passing of time. We buy into a lie that those we love will always be there for us, when that is just not how life works. A job offering may take a friend far away. Children grow up and leave the nest for opportunity. Divorce can destroy a family that once seemed inseparable. And, of course, death comes for us all at some point in time.

If we take each other for granted, then we have missed the fact that God has given us as gifts to each other and that is bad stewardship. One of my favorite movies is "Breakfast at Tiffany's," and in the closing scene the main character tries to explain that she belongs to nobody, only to hear her boyfriend proclaim to her that people do belong to each other. The reality is, in a family, we all belong to each other. I am yours, and you are mine. Next to life itself, those we love are by far God's greatest gifts to us.

Tell the ones you love, "Thank you." Thank them not only for what they do, but thank them for just being there. Never take them for granted, for life has made you a promise: they will not be there forever.

IDEA FOR RESPONSE

When the kids pick up their bedrooms or your spouse helps with the dishes this week, take time to sincerely thank them ... and not complain about how long it took them or how they didn't do it in the same way as you would have. Be grateful.

TAKE TIME TO REFLECT

Name 3 times when you were recognized for the work you did. What was said or done? How did it make you feel? How can you make others feel that way on a regular basis?

APPRECIATION

Lean on God

People were bringing children to him that he might touch them, but the disciples rebuked them. When Jesus saw this he became indignant and said to them, "Let the children come to me; do not prevent them, for the kingdom of God belongs to such as these. Amen, I say to you, whoever does not accept the kingdom of God like a child will not enter it." Then he embraced them and blessed them, placing his hands on them.

–Mark 10:13-16

Several years ago, there was a popular contemporary Christian song by Steven Curtis Chapman that contained the lyric, "God is God, and I am not." These words did not originate with Chapman, but it surely was a resounding message for a culture that too often upholds an ideal of success and accumulation of riches on one's own terms. Too often we buy into the lie that we are the gods of our own universe. We have the control and we decide what happens next in our lives.

However, the belief that we can depend on ourselves for everything in life is simply folly. In fact, Jesus asks us to come to him like children, not only dependent on God, but also cognizant of the fact that we never exist in the world alone. To be like a child is not to be immature, but rather, it is our maturity of faith that allows us to see our dependence on a loving Father.

Good stewards need to always remember that God is God and we are not. Stewardship is an acceptance that all we have and all we are is because of God. When we accept that, we no longer hold on to possessions and status too tightly. We learn to rest in Him when we are troubled, and call on Him when we are in need. As a community of children, we know who we really are. We cannot only renew our Church, we can make the world a better place. We just need to sing Chapman's lyric, and God will answer with a Bill Wither's lyric, "Lean On Me."

IDEA FOR RESPONSE

Spend 10 minutes praying for the will to "let go and let God."
Repeat those words several times during your prayer time.

TAKE TIME TO REFLECT

*Have you had times in your life when you truly "let go and
let God," giving all worry and control to Him? Did it feel
frightening, liberating, a little of both?*

DEPENDENT

Only God Is Perfect

For God is my witness, how I long for all of you with the affection of Christ Jesus. And this is my prayer: that your love may increase ever more and more in knowledge and every kind of perception, to discern what is of value, so that you may be pure and blameless for the day of Christ, filled with the fruit of righteousness that comes through Jesus Christ for the glory and praise of God.

–Philippians 1:8-11

Even though some people seem to live graced lives with little struggle, the truth is we all have struggles in life. Financial problems, health issues, emotions of fear and inadequacy, and even twists of fate are part of the human condition. The fact is that we are imperfect beings living in an imperfect world.

But there is the One who came into the world to fill the valleys and lower the mountains. He makes winding roads straight and rough roads smooth again. In fact, he makes new again that which was created at the beginning of time but then fell into disarray due to our sin. He is Jesus, and he not only makes all things new, he provides glimpses of perfection in our imperfect world.

With all that we have been given as gift, the greatest gift was the Incarnation, God made man. Through the birth of a baby, our reality was altered in this world forever, and a hope for life eternal with our God was possible. And now, we are called to spend our days as co-creators with God, cultivating all that has been given to us so the good work begun in us may be drawn near to completion.

We are imperfect beings in an imperfect world, but the One who makes all things perfect is doing great things in us.

IDEA FOR RESPONSE

Make a list of everything you are worrying about right now. Light a candle and consciously give your troubles to God.

TAKE TIME TO REFLECT

Have you seen glimpses of God when you or a loved one were going through a challenging time? Write about your experiences.

IMPERFECTION

A Thankful Heart

If there is any encouragement in Christ, any solace in love, any participation in the Spirit, any compassion and mercy, complete my joy by being of the same mind, with the same love, united in heart, thinking one thing. Do nothing out of selfishness or out of vainglory; rather, humbly regard others as more important than yourselves, each looking out not for his own interests, but [also] everyone for those of others.

Have among yourselves the same attitude that is also yours in Christ Jesus.
—Philippians 2:1-5

When I was younger, I used a reflection on youth retreats that depicted a disciple of Jesus and his concern about how much Jesus loved him. Several times over his life, the disciple would ask Jesus the question, "How much do you love me?" Each time Jesus would simply shake his head, wondering why the disciple would ask such a question. Then Jesus was arrested and sentenced to death, driving the disciple crazy with his inability to get an answer from Jesus. He was insecure and needed reassurance that the Jesus he loved cared for him just as much. Finally, he met Jesus before the moment of his execution and cried out to him to please ease his soul over the concern of how much he loved the disciple. Jesus then answered, "I love you more than you know. I love you this much," holding his arms out to his side as far as they would go. Then Jesus was seized while in that posture and nailed to a cross, making that gesture a permanent one for the disciple and everyone else to see.

I then would play a song entitled, "Thankful Heart," which contained the lyric, "I have a thankful heart, that you have given me, and it can only come from you." It was a moving reflection every time. After all that concern about how much the Master loved him, what else could he have but a profound sense of gratefulness? He received his answer, and with that answer, a symbol of the ultimate sacrifice of love.

Our gratefulness should overflow. Because of Jesus' death and resurrection, all things are made new and all things are possible. We are called to be thankful for all the gifts in our lives because the only reason any of the gifts matter is because of his ultimate gift: his life.

IDEA FOR RESPONSE
Take one of your crucifixes or crosses off the wall. Sit down and hold it in your lap. Thank Jesus for giving the ultimate sacrifice to demonstrate his love for you.

TAKE TIME TO REFLECT

Think of a time when someone asked you to do something but you declined because you were busy, too tired, or just didn't care. What do you think Jesus would tell you about the importance of sacrificing yourself for others?

Honor One Another

On the third day there was a wedding in Cana in Galilee, and the mother of Jesus was there. Jesus and his disciples were also invited to the wedding. When the wine ran short, the mother of Jesus said to him, "They have no wine." [And] Jesus said to her, "Woman, how does your concern affect me? My hour has not yet come." His mother said to the servers, "Do whatever he tells you."

–John 2:1-5

When I look back over my life, I see so many people who played an important role in my becoming who I am today. Some of them taught me about life, some shared with me stories that made me feel more human, and some showed me how God loves us by mirroring that unconditional love, even if it was imperfectly. At the top of the list of these influential people certainly are my parents, my teachers, my pastors, and now even my wife. I often tell my children that in many ways, we are the sum of our experiences, and certainly the experiences of family and friendship craft us profoundly.

These people are gifts. Plain and simple, they are some of the greatest gifts God will ever give to each of us. The commandment to honor thy mother and father has much greater implications for us than simply the need for us to obey parents or authority. Inherent in the commandment is the need for respect of anyone God has given to us in this life to mold and shape us. By honoring God's gift to us, we honor the One who created them.

Jesus received more at his birth than the gifts from the Magi. He received two earthly parents to care for him. They were certainly gifts worth more than any precious metals or oil. The story of the wedding feast in Cana speaks of his response to those gifts, particularly his mother. It was out of honor that he complied with Mary's request. One could say it was his great sense of stewardship that compelled him to honor the gift he had been given. By his actions, he gave us an example of how we must honor God's gifts of our loved ones. At the end of the day, these gifts are more valuable than a gift any earthly king might offer.

IDEA FOR RESPONSE

Choose 3 people who have played an important role in your life. Say an Our Father in thanksgiving for each of them.

TAKE TIME TO REFLECT

When was the last time you disrespected someone close to you? What was the reason? How did you express this disrespect? What affect did this have on your relationship?

HONOR

Thank-You Notes

As he continued his journey to Jerusalem, he traveled through Samaria and Galilee. As he was entering a village, ten lepers met [him]. They stood at a distance from him and raised their voice, saying, "Jesus, Master! Have pity on us!" And when he saw them, he said, "Go show yourselves to the priests." As they were going they were cleansed. And one of them, realizing he had been healed, returned, glorifying God in a loud voice; and he fell at the feet of Jesus and thanked him. He was a Samaritan. Jesus said in reply, "Ten were cleansed, were they not? Where are the other nine? Has none but this foreigner returned to give thanks to God?" Then he said to him, "Stand up and go; your faith has saved you."

–Luke 17:11-19

When I was young, my mother would make sure I wrote thank-you notes to anyone and everyone I could. I didn't mind writing them. It just seemed to me that she put so much pressure on me and made it seem they were the most important acts in the world.

When I was older, I realized that not everyone wrote thank-you notes. In fact, many people don't even offer a word of gratitude to your face while you are in the act of helping them! My assumption when I was a child that everyone understood the importance of gratitude was just that: an assumption, and an incorrect one.

We can often assume that in today's world this lack of thankfulness is even more profound than in the past. But Jesus healed ten lepers and only one felt the need to return and offer thanks, and he was a Samaritan, a foreigner, and societal outsider to the Jewish Jesus. But this one man, due to his movement of thanksgiving and faith, received something much more than a cure for an illness of the body. He received the salvation of his soul.

It is not so much that gratitude changes anything, but it is who we are as Christians. It is God's will for us to truly become living examples of the transforming power of thanksgiving, whether we have our mother telling us to give thanks or not.

IDEA FOR RESPONSE

Instead of just simply saying (or texting!) "thanks" to someone, make an effort to write a thank-you note to the people who helped you out at the parish food pantry, to the friend who surprised you with flowers for your birthday, or to the teacher who took your child under his or her wing.

TAKE TIME TO REFLECT

When have you failed to acknowledge someone for a gift they bought you or for a kind deed they did for you? How often do you thank God for all He provides?

All We Have Belongs to God

"What is your opinion? A man had two sons. He came to the first and said, 'Son, go out and work in the vineyard today.' He said in reply, 'I will not,' but afterwards he changed his mind and went. The man came to the other son and gave the same order. He said in reply, 'Yes, sir,' but did not go. Which of the two did his father's will?" They answered, "The first." Jesus said to them, "Amen, I say to you, tax collectors and prostitutes are entering the kingdom of God before you. When John came to you in the way of righteousness, you did not believe him; but tax collectors and prostitutes did. Yet even when you saw that, you did not later change your minds and believe him."

–Matthew 21:28-32

Remember a time when jealousy or envy reared its ugly head, and you wished you had something that someone else owned? Maybe it was a house, a car, a bank account, or even that luscious green lawn. All humans have had that feeling before and some of us more often than others. After the emotion hit you, hopefully you considered all the good gifts you did have in your life and gave thanks for them. Let's pray that you are still not hanging onto those feelings. Unfortunately, we do live in a world that seems to fuel those desires and push us toward wanting more and more.

But let's level the field here. Did you ever hear of someone who died and was able to take any of those things into the afterlife? The reality is that nothing we have in this life truly belongs to us. We come into this world with nothing. As time goes by, more gifts are entrusted to us, but we never truly own them. So whom do they belong to anyway?

Of course, you know the answer. All that we have has been entrusted to us by God: to be cherished, cultivated, and then given back to Him for His glory. God doesn't need any of these things, and we only need them short-term. All that we need long-term is God. If He is all we need in the end, I bet our lives would be more fruitful and happier if we focused on that now instead of later.

IDEA FOR RESPONSE

Take 10 items you "own" and give them to Goodwill, St. Vincent de Paul, or another charity. Free yourself ... at least a little bit at a time.

TAKE TIME TO REFLECT

Name 3 times when your pursuit of material possessions was your main focus. Did you pull away from God and other people?

Gotta Serve Somebody

"I tell you, make friends for yourselves with dishonest wealth, so that when it fails, you will be welcomed into eternal dwellings. The person who is trustworthy in very small matters is also trustworthy in great ones; and the person who is dishonest in very small matters is also dishonest in great ones. If, therefore, you are not trustworthy with dishonest wealth, who will trust you with true wealth? If you are not trustworthy with what belongs to another, who will give you what is yours? No servant can serve two masters. He will either hate one and love the other, or be devoted to one and despise the other. You cannot serve God and mammon."

–Luke 16:9-13

When the collection basket passes you by at church, what are you thinking? The reality is that your spiritual health is tied into what you think and what you do with your money. People like to say that stewardship doesn't have to do with money. But the reality is that money is such a strong force in our lives that if we relegate it to something outside of our spiritual journey, it has the potential to sneak up on us and take control before we know it.

In marriage, money is the source of most arguments and stress between spouses. The majority of big lottery winners find their lives in shambles just a few years after they cashed in the winning ticket. Credit card debt is a primary obstacle for many in trying to buy a house, car, or other primary item needed for basic living.

I heard a long time ago the P. T. Barnum quote, "Money is a terrible master but an excellent servant." The truth is that unless we exercise true dominion over our money and allow it to serve God's purpose, then we run the risk of waking up one day being enslaved by it. This does not only apply to what we give away to our parish, our community, or to charity. It applies to the money we use for shelter, food, and clothing. It applies to every dollar in our wallet and bank account. For it ALL belongs to God.

IDEA FOR RESPONSE

Do a true assessment of your finances. Know what you owe and to whom. Offer not only your treasure to God but your debts as well. You are not in this alone.

TAKE TIME TO REFLECT

Name 3 times when you squandered your money. Instead of buying a Starbucks' grande Caramel Macchiato every day or buying that item on Amazon, could you use those funds to help a charity or your church?

BELONGING

Many Gifts

When the time for Pentecost was fulfilled, they were all in one place together. And suddenly there came from the sky a noise like a strong driving wind, and it filled the entire house in which they were. Then there appeared to them tongues as of fire, which parted and came to rest on each one of them. And they were all filled with the holy Spirit and began to speak in different tongues, as the Spirit enabled them to proclaim.

Now there were devout Jews from every nation under heaven staying in Jerusalem. At this sound, they gathered in a large crowd, but they were confused because each one heard them speaking in his own language. They were astounded, and in amazement they asked, "Are not all these people who are speaking Galileans? Then how does each of us hear them in his own native language?"

–Acts 2:1-8

There are some things I miss now that my children are older. Fewer snuggles, fewer moments of awe and wonder, and fewer crazy questions that make me laugh. However, if I'm honest, there are some things I do not miss, especially the birthday party. I loved the aspect of celebrating my child's birth, but most years the party cost too much, involved too much stress, and resulted in a lot of presents that ended up in my garage. Today, nice dinners with family and friends and sharing time together have taken the place of the birthday party, and that is fine with me.

Centuries ago, God moved in such a profound way and sent His Holy Spirit upon us, imparting to the Church gifts that remain with us today. The first Pentecost was a first birthday party of sorts, with people gathered to celebrate their common faith in Jesus Christ. Of course, that party had none of the trappings of a child's event at Chuck E. Cheese's, but instead presented us all with generous gifts that could be used for the glory of God instead of the stuff children discard after a few weeks.

All year long, it is important to celebrate the Church that God has given to us. The generosity of God knows no limits, and the Holy Spirit is alive. It's just that the gifts from this celebration need to be used or the celebration will be hollow. The gifts are free to us even though they are priceless. It would be poor stewardship to toss them in the garage with all those toys that time forgot.

IDEA FOR RESPONSE

What is a talent God has given you? Musical skills, athleticism, artistic ability, the gift of cooking? Set aside some time to indulge in one of your talents, thanking God for the gift.

TAKE TIME TO REFLECT

Of all the talents you have been given, which is the one you use the most? How do you use it? How does putting your gift into action spread the Good News?

CELEBRATE

NOTES

NOTES

NOTES

Be Gracious

The 4th Characteristic
of an Everyday Steward

Be an Instrument of Grace

His father ordered his servants, 'Quickly bring the finest robe and put it on him;
put a ring on his finger and sandals on his feet. Take the fattened calf and
slaughter it. Then let us celebrate with a feast, because this son of mine was
dead, and has come to life again; he was lost, and has been found.' Then the
celebration began. Now the older son had been out in the field and, on his way
back, as he neared the house, he heard the sound of music and dancing. He
called one of the servants and asked what this might mean. The servant said to
him, 'Your brother has returned and your father has slaughtered the fattened
calf because he has him back safe and sound.' He became angry, and when he
refused to enter the house, his father came out and pleaded with him.

–Luke 15:22-28

Tom Chiarella wrote in his 2013 Esquire magazine article, "How to be Gracious and Why": "Graciousness looks easy, but of course it is not. Do not mistake mere manners for graciousness. Manners are rules. Helpful, yes. But graciousness reflects a state of being; it emanates from your inventory of self."

I think that all mature disciples of Jesus Christ should reflect a high level of graciousness in their life. It lends evidence to the joy of the Lord that resides in their heart and the grace that fills their being. Even in the ordinary circumstances of the day, good stewards display a giving demeanor that makes others take notice. Graciousness really makes a difference when it is displayed instead of anger, resentment, or ridicule. No story explains this more powerfully than the parable of the prodigal son.

In Jesus' parable, the father has every reason to share with his son his hurt and dissatisfaction upon his returning home after he wasted his inheritance and disgraced his family. Instead, his gracious response is overwhelming, so much so that the other son who has remained faithful becomes disgruntled. A gracious steward gives without asking why or care for the cost. And with grace comes mercy, not human justice. With true justice, we would all suffer. But with mercy comes love and the chance to begin again.

By developing graciousness in our lives, we become instruments of grace for the world around us. We provide glimpses of heaven and the love of the Father for His sons and daughters. And the feasts we prepare for those here on earth give them a taste of the heavenly banquet that awaits when we finally come home.

IDEA FOR RESPONSE

Identify one person in need of your forgiveness. Now, do what you know you should do.

TAKE TIME TO REFLECT

Name 3 times when someone has deeply disappointed you. Did you forgive them and let them have another chance? Was that difficult?

Listen First, Then Speak

[Jesus] asked them, "What are you discussing as you walk along?" They stopped, looking downcast. One of them, named Cleopas, said to him in reply, "Are you the only visitor to Jerusalem who does not know of the things that have taken place there in these days?" And he replied to them, "What sort of things?" They said to him, "The things that happened to Jesus the Nazarene, who was a prophet mighty in deed and word before God and all the people, how our chief priests and rulers both handed him over to a sentence of death and crucified him. But we were hoping that he would be the one to redeem Israel; and besides all this, it is now the third day since this took place. Some women from our group, however, have astounded us: they were at the tomb early in the morning and did not find his body; they came back and reported that they had indeed seen a vision of angels who announced that he was alive. Then some of those with us went to the tomb and found things just as the women had described, but him they did not see." And he said to them, "Oh, how foolish you are! How slow of heart to believe all that the prophets spoke! Was it not necessary that the Messiah should suffer these things and enter into his glory?" Then beginning with Moses and all the prophets, he interpreted to them what referred to him in all the scriptures. As they approached the village to which they were going, he gave the impression that he was going on farther. But they urged him, "Stay with us, for it is nearly evening and the day is almost over." So he went in to stay with them. And it happened that, while he was with them at table, he took bread, said the blessing, broke it, and gave it to them. With that their eyes were opened and they recognized him, but he vanished from their sight.

–Luke 24:17-31

The road to Emmaus is one of my favorite Gospel stories because it shows a Jesus who is masterful at reaching people. First, when he comes upon those walking on the road, he asks them what they are talking about and then asks them to explain. How often are we too eager to just start talking at people when we feel they need to hear what we have to say? Jesus offers an invitation for them to share first. Allowing them to share first opens them up for what Jesus will do next.

Second, Jesus takes time to interpret for them the words of the prophets. He gave them their turn and now it is his. Not only wise, but a movement of respect. After a long walk, they invite Jesus stay with them and dine. Third and finally, Jesus breaks bread with them and they are able to see that he is no ordinary traveler. He is the Risen One. He could have just told them who he was, but allowing them by their experience to uncover who he was had the greater impact.

Jesus demonstrated to us in these actions how to be gracious and impactful when sharing the Good News. If we are to be good stewards and fruitful disciples, then we must imitate him in this regard. No one can understand love without witnessing love. In this way, your words and deeds will become a pathway to Jesus for others.

IDEA FOR RESPONSE

Practice allowing others to speak first. Be patient and really listen to what they are saying before you try to talk.

TAKE TIME TO REFLECT

Have you encountered people who first talk about themselves before asking anything about you, if anything at all? What is your reaction to them in that conversation? Are you aware of when you have been the one dominating the conversation?

Generosity with No Limits

"You have heard that it was said, 'You shall love your neighbor and hate your enemy.' But I say to you, love your enemies, and pray for those who persecute you, that you may be children of your heavenly Father, for he makes his sun rise on the bad and the good, and causes rain to fall on the just and the unjust. For if you love those who love you, what recompense will you have? Do not the tax collectors do the same? And if you greet your brothers only, what is unusual about that? Do not the pagans do the same? So be perfect, just as your heavenly Father is perfect."

–Matthew 5:43-48

My pastor likes to say that his parents would always remind him to "leave a place you visited a little better than the way you found it." I have always tried to live by those words as well. The important word here is "tried," as I am sure that I have not always been successful.

The desire to always go a step further, to give even more than is required, is truly honorable. Jesus speaks to his disciples about this when he urges them to give more than what is asked and to travel two miles in service when all that was required of them is one. As disciples of Jesus, we are called to live the same way. It is fundamental to understanding a stewardship way of life.

True generosity has no limits. When we say that mature disciples are to answer the call of Jesus Christ regardless of the cost, we are inviting good stewards to embody this type of generosity. We can be the person who does not respond to the call, be the person who responds and gives what is required, or, finally, be the person who seeks to give above and beyond what is required. God doesn't just give us what we need, but He gives us more than we need. Made in His image, we are called to do the same. If we try to live in this manner every day, then we might just succeed in leaving this world a little better than the way we found it.

IDEA FOR RESPONSE

Find someone who needs your gracious generosity. Spend time with them and try to leave them better than you found them.

TAKE TIME TO REFLECT

Name 3 times when there was a limit to your generosity (time, money, patience, etc.). Why did you hold back? What more could you have given?

IMITATE

Is Tolerance a Substitute for Love?

"Teacher, which commandment in the law is the greatest?" He said to him, "You shall love the Lord, your God, with all your heart, with all your soul, and with all your mind. This is the greatest and the first commandment. The second is like it: You shall love your neighbor as yourself. The whole law and the prophets depend on these two commandments."

–Matthew 22:36-40

I read an interesting article about how tolerance has become a substitute for love. As Christians, we often talk about tolerance toward others when truly the call of Jesus Christ is to love others, not simply tolerate them. The truth is, tolerance is a lot easier than love.

In tolerance, we are asked to give nothing away. It costs us nothing to simply allow people to be who they are, where they are, and stay in the state in which they find themselves. Love requires us to step outside of our comfort zone and to offer a part of ourselves to others. This makes us vulnerable and open to possible pain and discomfort. Those whom we seek to love could take advantage of us. It is easy to see why tolerance seems a bit more popular these days.

Jesus could have tolerated the religious hypocrites of his day. He could have tolerated the Romans who oppressed the Jews. He could have simply tolerated the tax collectors, prostitutes, and outcasts of his day. Instead, he loved them. He made himself vulnerable and open to pain. When we look at the cross, we see what can be the true price for love. It is easy to see why a policy of tolerance looks more desirable to many.

IDEA FOR RESPONSE

Make a list of your pet peeves, like popping gum, talking loudly, cracking knuckles. Pray to God to make you less bothered by these inconsequential actions.

TAKE TIME TO REFLECT

Name 3 people in your life whom you simply tolerate instead of love. How can you change your view of that person so you see Jesus in him or her, allowing you to love them just as Jesus loves you just the way you are?

VULNERABILITY

We Are All Servants of God

"As for you, do not be called 'Rabbi.' You have but one teacher, and you are all brothers. Call no one on earth your father; you have but one Father in heaven. Do not be called 'Master'; you have but one master, the Messiah. The greatest among you must be your servant. Whoever exalts himself will be humbled; but whoever humbles himself will be exalted."

–Matthew 23:8-12

Over the years, we have had many great social events in our parish community. We have had socials for New Year's Eve, St. Patrick's Day, Mardi Gras, Our Lady of Guadalupe, Valentine's Day, and so many more. It seems we will use any excuse to have a party and enjoy each other's company. And for more than a decade, my pastor has been present at most of these events. What always tickles me is to see him in his clerics going around with a tray of entrees or desserts as he seeks to serve his parishioners. We have joked that his clothing does resemble that of a waiter in a fine restaurant. The only difference is no tips! Sorry, Monsignor.

To see a shepherd serve his sheep causes me to reflect on how we are all called to serve one another. We are called to a life of humility and service, giving of ourselves for the greater glory of God. When we seek to serve our brothers and sisters, the Jesus in us meets the Jesus in them.

In our everyday lives, we can find ways of serving others if we are mindful of the opportunities all around us. We must never fall into the trap of seeing others in terms of "us and them." In Christ, there is only us. In Christ, there is no Greek or Jew, servant or free. We are one. On this day, who will God place on your path for you to serve? Don't be fooled into thinking that all calls are for something grand. Sometimes, even a little dessert might be all it takes to show others they are loved.

IDEA FOR RESPONSE

Serve someone in a small way this week. Offer to pick up groceries for your elderly neighbor. Bring a meal to a sick parishioner. Pay someone a compliment.

TAKE TIME TO REFLECT

Write about a time when you were a guest at someone's home and they served you. Were you comfortable being taken care of? Are you more comfortable serving others?

SERVE

To Be Full of Grace

Mary said:
"My soul proclaims the greatness of the Lord;
my spirit rejoices in God my savior.
For he has looked upon his handmaid's lowliness;
behold, from now on will all ages call me blessed.
The Mighty One has done great things for me,
and holy is his name.
His mercy is from age to age
to those who fear him."

–Luke 1:46-50

I read once that to be a gracious person meant to walk softly, speak with intent, and to leave those you have met feeling that their lives were better that day because they encountered you. What a way to live!

But alas, living like that each and every day is so very hard. I hate to think that sometimes people I have encountered are happy to see me go, but I know that it is true. As Christians, we are graced people, but on some days, that grace can seem pretty hidden.

If you are looking for an example of gracious living, look no further than Our Lady. She answered the call regardless of the cost, and she lived her life with a great dignity in the face of horrible trials. She was a gracious host to the Incarnation in her womb, and she continues to invite us to get to know her Son better. She certainly embodies the definition of gracious living above.

We are called to always be ready and open to the call of her Son. He will bring us to those in need, seeking light in a world of darkness. Our hope must be then that after our encounter with another, they will feel enriched by our presence and the presence of Jesus.

IDEA FOR RESPONSE

Each morning for the next 3 days, sit in a quiet location, and recite the Hail Mary, asking Mary to fill you with grace.

TAKE TIME TO REFLECT

Think of 3 times when you had been less than gracious to your family, a friend, or a stranger. How did you treat them? How should you have treated them instead?

GRACE

Radical Stewardship

They stripped off his clothes and threw a scarlet military cloak about him. Weaving a crown out of thorns, they placed it on his head, and a reed in his right hand. And kneeling before him, they mocked him, saying, "Hail, King of the Jews!" They spat upon him and took the reed and kept striking him on the head. And when they had mocked him, they stripped him of the cloak, dressed him in his own clothes, and led him off to crucify him.

As they were going out, they met a Cyrenian named Simon; this man they pressed into service to carry his cross.

And when they came to a place called Golgotha (which means Place of the Skull), they gave Jesus wine to drink mixed with gall. But when he had tasted it, he refused to drink. After they had crucified him, they divided his garments by casting lots; then they sat down and kept watch over him there. And they placed over his head the written charge against him: This is Jesus, the King of the Jews.

–Matthew 27:28-37

I read a story recently about a teacher who donated a kidney to one of her former students. This tremendous act of selflessness came about because the young person had lost most of the function of his kidneys due to an illness. Literally, that teacher gave the gift of life to someone who wasn't her own child or another family member. This is certainly radical stewardship.

How far would you go to give of yourself so that another might live? Would you have to love him or her like your own child or parent? No one can deny it would be a difficult decision, especially if your giving put your own health at risk.

Reflecting on these things helps to provide some perspective on the crucifixion of Jesus. Not only did he suffer tremendously at the hands of the Romans, he gave his life for us so we might live forever. What does true stewardship look like? The cross is a symbol to us of total surrender. When we are called to give of ourselves in ordinary ways in daily life, we sometimes hesitate and think twice. Perhaps when we are unsure, we should look to the cross and there we can find our strength. And then when the call comes to truly sacrifice and place our trust in God, we may have already developed a lifestyle that makes responding, "Yes," that much easier.

IDEA FOR RESPONSE
Be conscience of all the good actions you see over the next 3 days. Jot them down and read through the list at the end of the week.

TAKE TIME TO REFLECT

Can you remember a time or two when someone was gracious for something you did for them ... and you had no idea it would mean so much? How did that gratefulness make you feel?

NO LIMIT

How Would You Rule Your Kingdom?

[Pilate] said to [Jesus], "Are you the King of the Jews?" Jesus answered, "Do you say this on your own or have others told you about me?" Pilate answered, "I am not a Jew, am I? Your own nation and the chief priests handed you over to me. What have you done?" Jesus answered, "My kingdom does not belong to this world. If my kingdom did belong to this world, my attendants [would] be fighting to keep me from being handed over to the Jews. But as it is, my kingdom is not here." So Pilate said to him, "Then you are a king?" Jesus answered, "You say I am a king. For this I was born and for this I came into the world, to testify to the truth. Everyone who belongs to the truth listens to my voice."

–John 18:33b-37

It would be kind of awesome to be a king or queen! Absolute rule, untold wealth, and people answering your every beck and call are things that wouldn't be half bad. Of course, I would be a benevolent monarch, and I would hope that all my subjects would love me. They could cheer me as I came out of the palace, and I think my popularity ratings in the polls would be through the roof. But if they weren't, that would be fine, too, because I would rule the kingdom. And that means no throwing me out of office. Talk about job security!

As great as that sounds, the King of kings could have had all that as well, but instead, he chose quite a different path. He gave up absolute rule so all his subjects could have the free will to choose to follow him. He gave up untold wealth so he could be treated like a common criminal and receive a death sentence. He gave up having servants at his disposal so he could be the servant of all his subjects himself. Yes, he was the King of kings, but he was nothing like a typical king. As much as I think it would be great to be a king myself, I would rather emulate this King instead.

Who would you rather be like? You could have it all or choose to give away everything. You could choose a path of luxury or a path of trial. You could be respected by many or find yourself in a culture that increasingly finds you objectionable. Who would you rather be like? Do you arrive at an answer quickly or do you need some time to think about it? The King of kings awaits your reply.

IDEA FOR RESPONSE

Pray the Our Father 3 times, pausing to reflect each time at the phrase, "Thy kingdom come."

TAKE TIME TO REFLECT

Have you ever held (or do you hold one now) a position of power, like a manager or head of a committee? How did you treat the people you supervised? In addition to giving directions, did you try to serve them in some way?

SERVANT

The Better Part

As they continued their journey he entered a village where a woman whose name was Martha welcomed him. She had a sister named Mary [who] sat beside the Lord at his feet listening to him speak. Martha, burdened with much serving, came to him and said, "Lord, do you not care that my sister has left me by myself to do the serving? Tell her to help me." The Lord said to her in reply, "Martha, Martha, you are anxious and worried about many things. There is need of only one thing. Mary has chosen the better part and it will not be taken from her."

–Luke 10:38-42

When we realize we are going to have company, my family and I swing into motion with a frenzy. No dust shall be present for our guests. The bathrooms will be spotless and toilets worthy of the name "throne." We must run to the store so that an endless supply of refreshments and snacks greet our distinguished guests. We never want to be seen as bad hosts. Of course, the real reason for all the commotion is we never want to be seen in our natural habitat of messy rooms and barren kitchens.

But what is real hospitality, a necessity for encouraging good stewardship and developing a sense of belonging? In the Gospel of Luke, Mary knew. Martha was so busy preparing and serving, while Mary simply sat with Jesus and listened to him. This is not to say that she did not prepare for her guest by making a proper place for gathering. But when a guest is already received, true hospitality begins with being present to and engaging him or her. Part of the message in this story is that we all need to pause and listen to the good news that Jesus preaches, but also we can learn a lesson about good hospitality from it as well.

How many times have we been more concerned with appearances and outward things than what we have inside each of us to share? Christian hospitality calls for the Jesus in me to meet with the Jesus in you. We are called to be fully present to one another, with no distractions of technology or the world standing in our way. This is choosing "the better part." For what does it profit a man if he has all the beer and wine in the world, and a spotless home with the greatest of technology, and loses his attention in the conversation with his brother or sister to the game on television? (Or something like that!)

IDEA FOR RESPONSE
Spend 1 day this week with no cell phone, TV, or Internet (except for your job). Detach and be more present (but don't get fired!).

TAKE TIME TO REFLECT

Think of an occasion when you were a guest and the host was frantically running around, refilling beverages, cleaning dishes, etc. Did you feel welcomed or more like a burden? How would you have preferred your host to act?

BEING PRESENT

Using Stones

[Stephen], filled with the holy Spirit, looked up intently to heaven and saw the glory of God and Jesus standing at the right hand of God, and he said, "Behold, I see the heavens opened and the Son of Man standing at the right hand of God." But they cried out in a loud voice, covered their ears, and rushed upon him together. They threw him out of the city, and began to stone him. The witnesses laid down their cloaks at the feet of a young man named Saul. As they were stoning Stephen, he called out, "Lord Jesus, receive my spirit." Then he fell to his knees and cried out in a loud voice, "Lord, do not hold this sin against them"; and when he said this, he fell asleep.

–Acts 7:55-60

After dealing with my children going through middle school, I am convinced those years are a time of real purgatory on earth. It is also a time that tests your faith in humanity, because you wonder at times, "Can people really be that mean to one another?"

It doesn't matter what crowd you are in. If you are cool or a nerd, tall or short, male or female, all will, at some time in middle school, be made to feel horrible. Didn't wear the right shoes today? Laughed too much at the joke? Made the mistake of telling the wrong person about a crush? For these and many more transgressions, you must be persecuted.

Most of us will not be persecuted and killed for our belief like Stephen. But what we choose to say and do to others can sometimes feel like being struck with hard stones, especially when we are young. At times in our lives, we find ourselves being hit hard by someone's lack of kindness or even hatred, and unfortunately, we sometimes find ourselves holding a stone.

I can't change those years of adolescence to make them easier, either for my own children or anyone else's. And I also know that ignorance and hateful behavior does not always stop when one gets older. People are mean at all ages. But only you and I have control of what we say and do. As good stewards, may we always be using stones to build bridges and shelter. May we never be found ready to hurl something at someone for any reason. And when we find ourselves on the receiving end of hate, may we have the strength to echo the words of Stephen, "Lord, do not hold this sin against them."

IDEA FOR RESPONSE
As you go through the next 3 days, think of your responses to situations. Don't let anger, resentment, or impatience be your first reactions.

TAKE TIME TO REFLECT

Think back to your middle school years. Were you ever the child who treated a classmate poorly? What did you do? If so, ask God for forgiveness. If you received the poor treatment, ask God to forgive your tormentors.

BUILD

NOTES

NOTES

NOTES

Be Committed

The 5th Characteristic
of an Everyday Steward

The Great Commission

The eleven disciples went to Galilee, to the mountain to which Jesus had ordered them. When they saw him, they worshiped, but they doubted. Then Jesus approached and said to them, "All power in heaven and on earth has been given to me. Go, therefore, and make disciples of all nations, baptizing them in the name of the Father, and of the Son, and of the holy Spirit, teaching them to observe all that I have commanded you. And behold, I am with you always, until the end of the age."

–Matthew 28:16-20

I remember watching part of a college graduation address where the speaker said, "With this degree you are commissioned to go into the world and make a difference." The imagery conjured up in my mind by the use of the word "commissioned" was pretty powerful. I thought about the commissioning of military officers and the responsibility they took on for the lives of not only their subordinates, but also the lives of those they protected. To me, the word meant something very serious and solemn. It meant huge responsibility and expectation.

At his ascension, Jesus gives what we call the Great Commission. The word "commission" makes this more than a suggestion or a hope. There is an expectation, a responsibility, and a mandate. Of course, did you wake up this morning thinking about how you would fulfill the Great Commission today?

Sharing the faith is not just something we should do; it is something we must do. The key is that you don't need to speak all the time to share. It will be through your life of stewardship that others will be able to see Jesus. By giving of yourself, by always responding to the call, and by surrendering all to God, you will lead others to become disciples, to seek out the sacraments, and to observe His teachings. Yes, by responding in full to the Great Commission, great things can happen.

IDEA FOR RESPONSE

Share some aspect of your stewardship journey on social media or with a friend in the next 2 to 3 days.

TAKE TIME TO REFLECT

Were you ever given a large, overwhelming assignment by a teacher or boss? How did you prepare your plan of action to commit to the work on a daily basis?

RESPOND

Letting Go

We know that all things work for good for those who love God, who are called according to his purpose. For those he foreknew he also predestined to be conformed to the image of his Son, so that he might be the firstborn among many brothers. And those he predestined he also called; and those he called he also justified; and those he justified he also glorified.

What then shall we say to this? If God is for us, who can be against us? He who did not spare his own Son but handed him over for us all, how will he not also give us everything else along with him?

–Romans 8:28-32

My wife is a big Dave Ramsey fan. She loves when he tells people that in order to pay down their debt, they need to sell so many of their possessions that the kids think that even they can be sold for the right price. He definitely sees earthly possessions as simply tools to be used and not possessed. This is a tough, countercultural message for sure in the eyes of the average American. Too often, our self-worth is derived from our wealth and the items we own. The size of our house, the brand of our car, and the quantity of our belongings are all gauges of success in our world. For Ramsey, not only can you not truly own anything if you owe money to others, it belongs to God anyway and is only given to us as stewards.

Could you sell all you have right now? Could you walk away from all that you have amassed and be truly free? When Jesus speaks of the merchant who sells all he has to obtain a pearl of great price, he calls us to see the pearl as the kingdom of heaven. Nothing on earth can rival the value of the kingdom. If that is true, why is it so hard to surrender everything to God to obtain it? It can be fear that keeps us from stepping out in faith. It can be selfishness that prevents us from letting go. Whatever it is, we must face the fact that we are possessed by it. The good news is that God does not expect us to conquer this obstacle on our own. But with God, all things are possible.

IDEA FOR RESPONSE

Walk into each room of your house and select at least one item to donate to charity.

TAKE TIME TO REFLECT

Name 3 times when you were scared to fully step out in your faith and clung to the material things and thoughts of this world. What are you afraid of? Can you commit to change your attitude?

SURRENDER

Better Today Than Yesterday

The scribes and the Pharisees brought a woman who had been caught in adultery and made her stand in the middle. They said to him, "Teacher, this woman was caught in the very act of committing adultery. Now in the law, Moses commanded us to stone such women. So what do you say?" They said this to test him, so that they could have some charge to bring against him. Jesus bent down and began to write on the ground with his finger. But when they continued asking him, he straightened up and said to them, "Let the one among you who is without sin be the first to throw a stone at her." Again he bent down and wrote on the ground. And in response, they went away one by one, beginning with the elders. So he was left alone with the woman before him. Then Jesus straightened up and said to her, "Woman, where are they? Has no one condemned you?" She replied, "No one, sir." Then Jesus said, "Neither do I condemn you. Go, [and] from now on do not sin any more."

–John 8:3-11

I had a conversation with my daughter about the responsibility she had to cultivate her God-given gifts and to give back with increase to God. She wanted to argue that just to be proficient in the use of those gifts was enough. Of course, she was just 15 at the time and as a typical teenager had no real desire to push much harder than necessary. I don't think she was ready to understand the value of perseverance and pushing onward to a goal. As she gets older and increases in maturity, I pray for her to really become committed to becoming the best she can be at whatever she does, because I know she has been given many gifts.

Being committed to growing in maturity as a disciple is important. This is a commitment to strive to be better today than we were yesterday ... and better tomorrow than we are today. We are also committed to getting back up and trying again when we fail to be the person God created us to be.

No one reading this is perfect. No one reading this has achieved a level of spiritual maturity to the point that we make the right call every time. But hopefully many of us are committed to working hard toward spiritual growth. Jesus asks each of us to work hard to become the saints God created us to be, just like he asked the woman caught in adultery to go forth and sin no more. He knew she had failed along the way, but not to get up and change her life would be the real sin. It is sin that keeps us from truly cultivating that which we have been given. However, God is committed to us and offers second chances. We need to be committed to Him.

IDEA FOR RESPONSE
Think of someone whom you have needlessly judged despite your own sinful ways. Ask God for forgiveness.

TAKE TIME TO REFLECT

When did you perform a task or function only to have it end up being a disaster? How did you grow from that experience? How can you apply the lessons you learned to your life as a maturing disciple?

From Sinner to Saint

Last of all, as to one born abnormally, he appeared to me. For I am the least of the apostles, not fit to be called an apostle, because I persecuted the church of God. But by the grace of God I am what I am, and his grace to me has not been ineffective. Indeed, I have toiled harder than all of them; not I, however, but the grace of God [that] is with me. Therefore, whether it be I or they, so we preach and so you believed.

−1 Corinthians 15:8-11

Don't you feel inspired when you hear a good conversion story? I know I do, especially tales of how people overcame addiction or despair to find satisfaction in the presence of God. It's the whole meaning of the hymn, "Amazing Grace": "I once was lost but now I'm found. Was blind, but now I see." The action there is from God, for it is He who finds us. He is the Good Shepherd who left the 99 to find that one lamb who could never find its way on its own. It is through grace that we can even turn at all, and it is grace that will lead us home.

That grace appears when we give ourselves over to God completely. We give God our whole heart, mind, and soul, and He turns that which was broken into something beautiful. I love St. Paul's statement of faith: "But by the grace of God I am what I am." Before that grace, Paul persecuted the followers of Jesus, and without that grace, he would have continued to live his evil life. To those who cannot understand how someone so horrible and full of sin can become a saint, his statement, in a way, alludes to the fact that he can't believe it either.

When we, as disciples of Jesus, decide to live a stewardship way of life, it only becomes transformational when we offer everything to him. No one is saying you are living a life like the old Saul and you need to turn to Jesus. Hopefully you have already turned to him. But have you really let go of it all? Do you still think in terms of what is for God and what is for you? Whatever you still hold onto is worthless compared to the grace offered to you for giving it up. Don't hold out any longer, for grace will lead you home.

IDEA FOR RESPONSE

Listen to a recording of "Amazing Grace." Close your eyes, take slow, deep breaths, and listen to the words, reflecting on how God has found you after a time of being lost.

TAKE TIME TO REFLECT

Name at least 3 ways how your relationship with God has transformed your life. What sinful actions or attitudes have you left in the past? How has your faith grown?

The Long Journey

[Jesus] said to them, "But who do you say that I am?" Peter said in reply, "The Messiah of God." He rebuked them and directed them not to tell this to anyone.

He said, "The Son of Man must suffer greatly and be rejected by the elders, the chief priests, and the scribes, and be killed and on the third day be raised."

Then he said to all, "If anyone wishes to come after me, he must deny himself and take up his cross daily and follow me. For whoever wishes to save his life will lose it, but whoever loses his life for my sake will save it."

–Luke 9:20-24

There once lived a man named Alvin Straight. He lived in Iowa. His brother Henry lived in Wisconsin. Alvin loved his brother. In 1994, at the age of 80, Henry had a stroke. Alvin, in his late 70s himself, could not imagine not being there for the brother he loved, but he had no driver's license and was uneasy about forms of public transportation. So Alvin climbed aboard his riding lawnmower and set out on a 240-mile journey that would eventually lead him to Henry.

The road was anything but easy, going all that way on a lawnmower. He broke down several times. He ran out of money. Day after day passed with Alvin traveling at a speed of 5 mph most of the time. But nothing could have stopped Alvin from getting to his destination. The love of his brother was a greater power than all the hardships combined. After nearly six weeks, he finally got to his brother.

Alvin's story is an amazing one. What Jesus asks us to do because of our love of him is amazing as well. We are to take up our cross and follow him, giving away all we have, even our very lives, so that we may be free to follow. The road is not easy, and all of us fall and end up sitting on the side of the road. But our love of Jesus should be stronger than any force we could meet up with along the way. His love for us was stronger than anything he faced along his journey with the cross. Just like Alvin, nothing could have stopped Jesus from completing his journey. Just like Alvin, we are called to make a similar journey and stay on course, regardless of the cost.

IDEA FOR RESPONSE
Within the next few days, make a journey to a church or shrine to visit with Jesus outside of the liturgy.

TAKE TIME TO REFLECT

When have you gone to great lengths to travel somewhere? Driving in a snowstorm ... taking several connecting flights ... missing connections. Did you feel like giving up? What made you continue? Why do you continue your faith journey?

PERSEVERE

Liberated to Believe

As they were proceeding on their journey someone said to Jesus, "I will follow you wherever you go." Jesus answered him, "Foxes have dens and birds of the sky have nests, but the Son of Man has nowhere to rest his head." And to another he said, "Follow me." But he replied, "[Lord], let me go first and bury my father." But he answered him, "Let the dead bury their dead. But you, go and proclaim the kingdom of God." And another said, "I will follow you, Lord, but first let me say farewell to my family at home." [To him] Jesus said, "No one who sets a hand to the plow and looks to what was left behind is fit for the kingdom of God."

–Luke 9:57-62

The world is a very busy place. Our lives are sometimes very complicated. Everywhere we turn, there are distractions. Add to all this the increasing number of people with virtually no attention span or diagnosed ADD, and you have a reality where it can be quite hard to stay focused and committed to any task at hand.

When you were called to follow Jesus, he knew that the call came in the midst of all this chaos. He understood that you would be pulled in every direction. That is why he urges you, as he did his first disciples, not to look behind, but to forge ahead, proclaiming the Good News to all who can hear. As Dietrich Bonhoeffer, the German Lutheran, described it in "The Cost of Discipleship," Jesus asks for a "single-minded obedience."

Bonhoeffer wrote, "The actual call of Jesus and the response of single-minded obedience have an irrevocable significance. By means of them Jesus calls people into an actual situation where faith is possible. For that reason his call is an actual call and he wishes it so to be understood, because he knows that it is only through actual obedience that a man can become liberated to believe" (Translated by R. H. Fuller. New York: Macmillan, 1963).

The reality is that we cannot, on our own, believe in and follow Jesus without turning ourselves over to him completely. The aspect of this that the world will never understand is that through giving all over to God, a person finds true freedom. By forsaking everything else for God, we gain everything. Good stewardship and mature discipleship needs this "single-minded obedience" to flourish. Without it, we will be constantly distracted and tempted to change course. A person with severe ADD may need a prescription. Any Christian seeking to follow Jesus needs something, too: the grace that comes from giving over one's self to God.

IDEA FOR RESPONSE
Try adding to your morning routine a quick prayer offering all you do and say that day for the glory of God.

TAKE TIME TO REFLECT

Name 3 things (emotions, material goods, thoughts, behaviors, etc.) that can preoccupy your head and heart. Where do your thoughts go when you aren't faced with distractions?

OBEY

Regardless of the Cost

Jesus replied, "A man fell victim to robbers as he went down from Jerusalem to Jericho. They stripped and beat him and went off leaving him half-dead. A priest happened to be going down that road, but when he saw him, he passed by on the opposite side. Likewise a Levite came to the place, and when he saw him, he passed by on the opposite side. But a Samaritan traveler who came upon him was moved with compassion at the sight. He approached the victim, poured oil and wine over his wounds and bandaged them. Then he lifted him up on his own animal, took him to an inn and cared for him. The next day he took out two silver coins and gave them to the innkeeper with the instruction, 'Take care of him. If you spend more than what I have given you, I shall repay you on my way back.'"

–Luke 10:30-35

What does it mean to give of yourself completely, without reservation, without fear, and without a concern for the cost? Should it matter if the person who needs us is unlike us in skin color, religion, or nationality? What does real mercy look like?

Jesus answered these questions beautifully in perhaps the greatest of the stewardship parables, the story of the Good Samaritan. Here a Judean traveler has been attacked, beaten, and left for dead on the side of the road. Others see him, but the cost to them to stop and help is too great. It is a Samaritan, one who is despised by most in the area, who stops, and gives of his time, talent, and treasure to help the poor victim.

Where the Samaritan was going we cannot know for sure, but he stopped to give his time to the beaten man. Using oil and wine, he bandaged the wounds. Not everyone has the knowledge and skills to care for someone in this manner. Here, he gave of his talent. Then he placed the man on his own animal and carried him to an inn the rest of the day. The following day he pays the innkeeper, yet leaves explaining that if the payment is not enough, when he travels back on through he will repay him whatever the cost. Of course, here he shares his treasure.

The sharing of these things is profound enough, but it is the statement of his willingness to pay whatever the balance is that elevates this tale to an ultimate example of stewardship. The Samaritan does not care how high the cost. He will give whatever is needed. This is mature discipleship, to respond to the call of Jesus Christ regardless of the cost. This is true stewardship.

IDEA FOR RESPONSE
Try to increase your offering to your church, your family, or to a charity this week by just a few dollars or a few extra minutes. Work towards giving more and more of yourself.

TAKE TIME TO REFLECT

When have you stopped in your tracks to help someone in need ... maybe a hurt child, someone broken down on the side of the road, or a struggling mom in the grocery store? How did you help? What was their reaction?

Patience Is a Virtue

"Gird your loins and light your lamps and be like servants who await their master's return from a wedding, ready to open immediately when he comes and knocks. Blessed are those servants whom the master finds vigilant on his arrival. Amen, I say to you, he will gird himself, have them recline at table, and proceed to wait on them. And should he come in the second or third watch and find them prepared in this way, blessed are those servants. Be sure of this: if the master of the house had known the hour when the thief was coming, he would not have let his house be broken into. You also must be prepared, for at an hour you do not expect, the Son of Man will come."

–Luke 12:35-40

Patience is a virtue. At least that's what they say. You might think Geoffrey Chaucer in "The Canterbury Tales" first used the saying. There he wrote, "Patience is a great virtue of perfection." However, William Langland first used the saying in 1370 in his poem, "The Vision of Piers." The poem was in Middle English, so the saying reads, "Suffraunce is a soverayn virtue." But you get the picture, and you have something to store away for your next trivia contest.

Jesus hadn't read Chaucer or Langland when he was talking to his disciples about the servant who begins to act improperly towards his charges because he believes there has been a delay in the master's return. But Jesus was talking about the values of patience and commitment. He was urging them to stay ready and keep working to spread the Good News. It is easy for a person to get complacent and let down one's guard. It is easy for a person to get tired of waiting and then turn to other sources of satisfaction.

The stewardship way of life is just that: a way of life. It is 24/7. We sometimes want to reduce it to a series of activities or take a break from giving of ourselves so much. We are not only talking about the Second Coming of Jesus Christ, but the ways that Jesus comes to us daily in the form of people in need. If we are not vigilant, we run the risk of being found asleep or, even worse, when the Master comes to call.

A virtue is a trait or quality that we see as morally good or a necessary component for a moral life. Patience is important because staying the course and carrying the cross of Jesus is not easy. But Jesus, and Chaucer and Langland, are sure the reward at the end of the road is well worth it.

IDEA FOR RESPONSE
The next time you feel yourself about to lose your patience with your kids, spouse, co-worker, or even a stranger, take a deep breath and count to 10.

TAKE TIME TO REFLECT

When have you treated your faith more of as a duty instead of a way of life? How can you better stay the course?

VIGILANCE

The Prize

For I am already being poured out like a libation, and the time of my departure is at hand. I have competed well; I have finished the race; I have kept the faith. From now on the crown of righteousness awaits me, which the Lord, the just judge, will award to me on that day, and not only to me, but to all who have longed for his appearance.

At my first defense no one appeared on my behalf, but everyone deserted me. May it not be held against them! But the Lord stood by me and gave me strength, so that through me the proclamation might be completed and all the Gentiles might hear it. And I was rescued from the lion's mouth. The Lord will rescue me from every evil threat and will bring me safe to his heavenly kingdom. To him be glory forever and ever. Amen.

–2 Timothy 4:6-8, 16-18

There was a movie a few years back entitled "Fever Pitch," where Jimmy Fallon played a devoted Red Sox fan. He was so loyal and consumed by the Red Sox that it was a huge obstacle to any romantic relationship he tried to start. In the end, he found a partner in a woman, played by Drew Barrymore, who was able to deal with his devotion once he showed he was willing to give up his season tickets for her. In fact, she came to love how he cared about something so much, realizing few people care that much about anything.

Loyalty to a sports team can be tested when wins are hard to come by. But true fans never forsake their teams. They cheer them on through the good times and the bad.

The extreme loyalty of the most faithful sports fan gives us only a glimpse of the loyalty God has for us. If everyone chooses to desert us, God remains faithful to His own. This reality should have such an impact on our lives because we never need to fear the obstacles and trials ahead. The life of a disciple is not an easy one. People will sometimes find our faithfulness unsettling, or it may make them feel uncomfortable. They may choose to walk away rather than hear about this Jesus who seems all consuming. But the loyalty and faithfulness of God can be your strength. In Him, you will find the strength to run the race and reach the finish line.

And when you cross that finish line, God will be there: your coach, your teammate, and your greatest fan. Think about what happened to the Red Sox after so many years of disappointment. Even when it seems you have no chance to win, God knows if you stick to the game plan, the prize will be yours.

IDEA FOR RESPONSE

Make a list of the people who support you in your Everyday Stewardship journey. How can you in turn support them?

TAKE TIME TO REFLECT

Have you ever met anyone who was clearly uncomfortable when you talked about your faith and God? How did you respond?

A Small Amount

The apostles said to the Lord, "Increase our faith." The Lord replied, "If you have faith the size of a mustard seed, you would say to [this] mulberry tree, 'Be uprooted and planted in the sea,' and it would obey you.

"Who among you would say to your servant who has just come in from plowing or tending sheep in the field, 'Come here immediately and take your place at table'? Would he not rather say to him, 'Prepare something for me to eat. Put on your apron and wait on me while I eat and drink. You may eat and drink when I am finished'? Is he grateful to that servant because he did what was commanded? So should it be with you. When you have done all you have been commanded, say, 'We are unprofitable servants; we have done what we were obliged to do.'"

–Luke 17:5-10

Some weeks seem to move steadily downhill as soon as they start. Your boss hits you with some hard criticism. Driving around town seems to be a constant experience of getting cut off and tailgated. The waiter at the restaurant felt pretty sure that your burnt and dried out lunch was not his problem. The kids didn't plan ahead once again, and the entire science fair project is due: tomorrow!

Then an angel of God in the form of a friend, acquaintance, or stranger says one nice thing, does one good deed, or offers a small gift of kindness, and suddenly the entire week changes. The power of good is always able to defeat the bad in our lives, but it is amazing that so much bad can be overcome by such a small amount of good — truly amazing.

Jesus told us that with a little faith, we could accomplish great things. The faith of a mustard seed can move mountains or uproot a tree from the earth and replant it in the sea. It does not take much to make a big difference in the world.

If we apply this understanding to stewardship, then we can see that small gifts of time, talent, or treasure can yield great harvests. Yes, we are called to offer all we have back to God and His people, but that does not change the fact that through small offerings of ourselves we can change the greater reality in the lives of many.

For many years, I had a tapestry hanging in my office with a quote from the Quaker theologian, Rufus Jones. He said, "I pin my hopes to quiet processes and small circles, in which vital and transforming events take place." With our stewardship, we have the chance to transform the world around us, even when it seems like what we can offer is so very small at the time.

IDEA FOR RESPONSE
Be an angel to a friend or family member who is having a difficult time. Call, write, email, or text them to let them know they are in your prayers.

TAKE TIME TO REFLECT

Name 3 times in your life when God's love for you was apparent and He gave you the strength to carry on. Did other people notice your courage? Did you praise God for His support?

NOTES

NOTES

NOTES

Be
Accountable

*The 6th Characteristic
of an Everyday Steward*

Work Together for God

"If you love me, you will keep my commandments. And I will ask the Father, and he will give you another Advocate to be with you always, the Spirit of truth, which the world cannot accept, because it neither sees nor knows it. But you know it, because it remains with you, and will be in you. I will not leave you orphans; I will come to you. In a little while the world will no longer see me, but you will see me, because I live and you will live. On that day you will realize that I am in my Father and you are in me and I in you. Whoever has my commandments and observes them is the one who loves me. And whoever loves me will be loved by my Father, and I will love him and reveal myself to him."

–John 14:15-21

My children could never succeed without their mother and me. That isn't me thinking too much of ourselves. It is just a fact. No one can find success in life in total isolation. I could never have become who I am today without my parents, various teachers and mentors, and my wife. Truth be told, I probably owe a lot of who I am to my children as well.

I can only imagine the fear and concern of the first disciples when it was apparent that Jesus was not going to be with them much longer. Some probably thought since Jesus had risen from the dead, he might just live with them in the same way forever. But Jesus tried to calm their fears by assuring them, "I will not leave you orphans." He said he would continue to come to them and that he would send the Spirit to be with them at all times. They would not have to continue what he had started and preach the Good News to the ends of the earth on their own.

We may sometimes feel that we are alone. We may at times try to do too much or show others that we are independent and strong. However, without the help of others, without the help of God, true success will always elude us. Our actions and words can become empty. The gifts we have received can either be cultivated in secret and in the shadows, or we can welcome the help that God provides in His Spirit, His community, and the sacraments He gave us. By working together, the world will truly know the power of the risen Lord.

IDEA FOR RESPONSE

Name 3 events you have worked on with other people where you really came together and made a difference.

TAKE TIME TO REFLECT

When have you tried to tackle a task on your own only to come up short? How could other people have helped you? Why didn't you ask for help?

TEAMWORK

Rules Are a Good Thing?

"Do not think that I have come to abolish the law or the prophets. I have come not to abolish but to fulfill. Amen, I say to you, until heaven and earth pass away, not the smallest letter or the smallest part of a letter will pass from the law, until all things have taken place. Therefore, whoever breaks one of the least of these commandments and teaches others to do so will be called least in the kingdom of heaven. But whoever obeys and teaches these commandments will be called greatest in the kingdom of heaven. I tell you, unless your righteousness surpasses that of the scribes and Pharisees, you will not enter into the kingdom of heaven."

–Matthew 5:17-20

I saw a slogan once for an Internet start-up: "There is one rule; there are no rules." In fact, when I searched for this slogan again online, I was surprised at all of the variations on the "no rules" sentiment. Apparently, even Justin Bieber has a documented quote: "I want my world to be fun. No parents, no rules, no nothing. Like, no one can stop me. No one can stop me." Wow. My own kids seldom read my reflections. If they are reading this one, don't get any ideas!

Of course, a society without laws or rules will not exist for very long. The laws of a society are there to protect us from perhaps our greatest enemy: ourselves. We can't just do whatever we feel like. We will eventually hurt others or ourselves. The laws of God and His Church have the same effect. Sinful and imperfect people need parameters. Christians who choose sin or their own will over God's commandments not only break the relationship they have with their God, but they hurt others and diminish the body of Christ.

A stewardship way of life asks of us to live in a certain manner. We sometimes think that our cultivation of gifts and giving them back with increase to God is for God's sake. God's commands do not benefit God, for God is complete and perfect without need for increase. But this way of life is for the benefit of His creation. There is no power struggle here between a God of rules and His children. The cross bears witness to that. Instead, God's "rules" prevent us from destroying ourselves, and give us a path so we may flourish. Whether you are an ordinary Joe or an ordinary Bieber, following God's commands will lead to the real satisfaction in this gift of life.

IDEA FOR RESPONSE
Read Matthew 5, 6, and 7 about God's various teachings.

TAKE TIME TO REFLECT

Do you tend to break different rules from God or the same ones over and over again?

The Weight of Our Actions

We give thanks to God always for all of you, remembering you in our prayers, unceasingly calling to mind your work of faith and labor of love and endurance in hope of our Lord Jesus Christ, before our God and Father, knowing, brothers loved by God, how you were chosen. For our gospel did not come to you in word alone, but also in power and in the holy Spirit and [with] much conviction. You know what sort of people we were [among] you for your sake.

–1 Thessalonians 1:2-5

Many years ago, during faith formation in my parish, one of the children wrote something that wasn't very nice on a textbook that belonged to someone else. Being the pastoral associate that oversaw the program, I began the investigation immediately. Slowly I began eliminating suspects until it became obvious who the perpetrator was. He denied he was the one, but after much pressure he broke down and confessed. Of course, I derived no satisfaction from finding out the culprit. Of course, it was my own son.

My son didn't want to come clean because he naturally feared what I would say and do when I found out. He also knew that our pastor would find out as well. He felt accountable for his actions and that made it very difficult for him. He realized he let himself, others that loved him, and God down. It was a lesson learned that wasn't much fun to go through. What I was grateful for was the fact that he felt the weight of what he had done. If he hadn't, things would have been very different.

That was a long time ago and when I reflect on it, I think about how often we all do things we regret and then have to face the consequences. But that's what being accountable is all about. We are accountable to those we love, to our neighbor, and to our God. When we begin to slide into a worldview that focuses too much on ourselves, we can easily make decisions that hurt others. We must always seek to do what is good in the eyes of God and that respects others. When we are children, this is easier said than done. Alright, let's be honest — it isn't always so easy as adults either.

IDEA FOR RESPONSE

Think of a bad habit you want to break. Ask your family and friends to hold you accountable when they see you stumbling.

TAKE TIME TO REFLECT

Name 3 times when you've said or done something you regretted. If it involved another person, did you apologize right away? Did you hope no one would ever find out? Did you do something to cover up what you had done?

CONFESS

No "I" in Team

Since, then, we have the same spirit of faith, according to what is written, "I believed, therefore I spoke," we too believe and therefore speak, knowing that the one who raised the Lord Jesus will raise us also with Jesus and place us with you in his presence. Everything indeed is for you, so that the grace bestowed in abundance on more and more people may cause the thanksgiving to overflow for the glory of God.

Therefore, we are not discouraged; rather, although our outer self is wasting away, our inner self is being renewed day by day. For this momentary light affliction is producing for us an eternal weight of glory beyond all comparison, as we look not to what is seen but to what is unseen; for what is seen is transitory, but what is unseen is eternal.

–2 Corinthians 4:13-18

I have coached all three of my children in soccer at some time in their lives. I loved teaching them and their teammates the importance of functioning as one unit. If we were not all moving together toward victory, we would all find ourselves together in defeat. We used to go through one drill I called the "human foosball." We would scrimmage with players in lines like on a foosball table. If you ever got too far behind or too far ahead of those in your line, play would stop and the ball would go to the other team. The goal was to help build an awareness of where your teammates were on the pitch and to teach the lesson that no one player is a team onto themselves.

As disciples and stewards, we sometimes find ourselves far behind or maybe even too far ahead. As a consequence, our actions either hinder the ability of the Body of Christ to evangelize and pass on the faith to a new generation or present the Church as an entity that sees itself as judgmental or too holy to be in the world. We are called to community, and in that community, we must be aware of our brothers and sisters in the faith. At times, we need to help them grow in their faith. Other times, we need to slow down and realize that we cannot change the world on our own. We all have unique gifts we are called to share, and we can only bear true witness to the power of the Body of Christ when we are all moving together and making each other strong.

IDEA FOR RESPONSE

Make a list of those who assist you in your spiritual life (family, friends, coworkers, etc.). Thank God for their presence and ask Him to bless them.

TAKE TIME TO REFLECT

How do you fit into the Body of Christ? What 3 gifts do you have that can make the Church stronger?

UNITED

No Volunteers Needed

The body, however, is not for immorality, but for the Lord, and the Lord is for the body; God raised the Lord and will also raise us by his power.

Do you not know that your bodies are members of Christ? But whoever is joined to the Lord becomes one spirit with him. Avoid immorality. Every other sin a person commits is outside the body, but the immoral person sins against his own body. Do you not know that your body is a temple of the holy Spirit within you, whom you have from God, and that you are not your own? For you have been purchased at a price. Therefore glorify God in your body.

–1 Corinthians 6:13c-15a, 17-20

Can you imagine what kind of response I would get if I asked my three children, "Who would like to volunteer to clean up the kitchen after dinner today?" Six eyeballs staring at me like I had two heads! If I couch my request in terms of volunteerism, I have suggested that they don't have any real ownership in this matter. Perhaps they do sometimes think that their mother and I are simply hired hands to take care of them, but rest assured, I have not received a paycheck for services rendered lately.

When you and I give a donation of blood, we volunteer our time and blood to the Red Cross. The Red Cross does not employ most of us, nor do we own a part of the Red Cross. We can only volunteer ourselves for the cause.

As parishioners, we are part of a parish family. We belong to our parish community. We do not visit on a Sunday morning, since we cannot visit a place that is home. The call of the body of Christ occurs in every parish, and our response should be that of the psalmist, "Here am I, Lord; I come to do your will." Real stewardship never counts the cost and never asks for volunteers. We step forward because we belong to something greater than ourselves, and the head of that community is Jesus. After dinner at my house, someone needs to clean up the kitchen. In your parish community, someone needs to respond to the call of Jesus. In both cases, no volunteers are needed. We will rely on family instead.

IDEA FOR RESPONSE

Search your parish bulletin or website for some need you can help fulfill. If you are already very involved, look for something short term or a single event.

TAKE TIME TO REFLECT

Do you ever see divisions between different groups in your parish community? What can you do to build a stronger faith family?

FAMILY

Sharing the Good News

There was a woman afflicted with hemorrhages for twelve years. She had suffered greatly at the hands of many doctors and had spent all that she had. Yet she was not helped but only grew worse. She had heard about Jesus and came up behind him in the crowd and touched his cloak. She said, "If I but touch his clothes, I shall be cured." Immediately her flow of blood dried up. She felt in her body that she was healed of her affliction. Jesus, aware at once that power had gone out from him, turned around in the crowd and asked, "Who has touched my clothes?" But his disciples said to him, "You see how the crowd is pressing upon you, and yet you ask, 'Who touched me?'" And he looked around to see who had done it. The woman, realizing what had happened to her, approached in fear and trembling. She fell down before Jesus and told him the whole truth. He said to her, "Daughter, your faith has saved you. Go in peace and be cured of your affliction."

–Mark 5:25-34

As the baptized, we are called into community, and we are strongest when all members have full faith in Jesus Christ. When one of us falters or begins to doubt his or her faith, that is when our faith is to be shared freely as a source of strength. If we hold our faith inside, then those around us will miss a chance to be edified and strengthened by our witness.

We can give freely of our money, our time, and our talents, but still not share our faith with those around us. This hinders the Body of Christ's ability to evangelize and spread the Good News. It also helps to keep members of that Body weak, because without the chance to hear our stories of faith, those with the need to hear can remain discouraged and lost.

Faith is a gift from God to us, just like any other. We are called to cultivate our faith and grow it into abundance. If we do not share it with others, then why grow it at all? We are not saved because we have more faith than someone else. We are no better off with storage bins filled with knowledge, devotion, and faith experience than a baby on its day of baptism. The difference between the baby and us is that we have something now to share and the responsibility to do so.

IDEA FOR RESPONSE

If you want to delve deeper into your faith, connect with a spiritual coach or director.

TAKE TIME TO REFLECT

When have you connected with someone whose faith was on fire, even though they were going through a difficult time? How did they inspire you?

TESTIFY

Choose Your Acquaintances Wisely

Then James and John, the sons of Zebedee, came to him and said to him, "Teacher, we want you to do for us whatever we ask of you." He replied, "What do you wish [me] to do for you?" They answered him, "Grant that in your glory we may sit one at your right and the other at your left." Jesus said to them, "You do not know what you are asking. Can you drink the cup that I drink or be baptized with the baptism with which I am baptized?" They said to him, "We can." Jesus said to them, "The cup that I drink, you will drink, and with the baptism with which I am baptized, you will be baptized; but to sit at my right or at my left is not mine to give but is for those for whom it has been prepared." When the ten heard this, they became indignant at James and John. Jesus summoned them and said to them, "You know that those who are recognized as rulers over the Gentiles lord it over them, and their great ones make their authority over them felt. But it shall not be so among you. Rather, whoever wishes to be great among you will be your servant; whoever wishes to be first among you will be the slave of all. For the Son of Man did not come to be served but to serve and to give his life as a ransom for many."

–Mark 10:35-45

Do you remember a time when you felt important because of your association with someone else? Maybe it was in school and you got to hang with the cool kids. Maybe it was being asked to lunch by company leadership. Perhaps it even happened at church when you spent more time than usual with your new friend, the pastor.

As humans, we sometimes think our friends, acquaintances, or colleagues elevate our status. It is true that whom we surround ourselves with is important. Parents are correct when they tell their children to hang out with the right crowd. Successful people do most times achieve success by surrounding themselves with other successful people. But the reality is that who we really are is mostly determined by our own actions, not the actions of others.

The trap for a Christian is the belief that it is enough to simply associate with Jesus Christ. James and John thought something similar in Mark's Gospel when they asked for seats of prominence next to Jesus in his coming kingdom. But Jesus explained to them that essentially it is not who you associate with that makes all the difference, it is becoming like those with whom you associate. We are called to become Jesus in the world, to be a servant of all, just as he chose to do.

I bet it was great for the first disciples to hang with Jesus, the savior of the world. But in the end, the goal was not for others to look at them and think they were so wonderful. The goal was for others to look at them and see not them, but only Jesus. If that can happen to us, now, that's cool.

IDEA FOR RESPONSE
Spend some time in self-reflection thinking about the people with whom you associate.

TAKE TIME TO REFLECT

When have you acted differently around someone you wanted to impress? How did you compromise your principles? Did you end up being friends with that person?

A Fruitless Fig Tree

[Jesus] told them this parable: "There once was a person who had a fig tree planted in his orchard, and when he came in search of fruit on it but found none, he said to the gardener, 'For three years now I have come in search of fruit on this fig tree but have found none. [So] cut it down. Why should it exhaust the soil?' He said to him in reply, 'Sir, leave it for this year also, and I shall cultivate the ground around it and fertilize it; it may bear fruit in the future. If not you can cut it down.'"

–Luke 13:6-9

What happens when people are allowed to do anything they want without any repercussions? A monster is created. Have you seen the parents who never correct or chastise their children? How about the person who keeps bullying others without anybody standing up to him? Then there are institutions like banks and corporations that continually scam the public without even so much as getting a slap on the wrist! The problem is a lack of accountability. Also, unfortunately, without accountability a person has no chance of changing.

Oftentimes without a person or community that holds them accountable, people never find the incentive to change. Even after one is held accountable, there should be assistance in trying to turn over a new leaf and become better.

Being accountable is a primary characteristic of an Everyday Steward. We must always be willing to accept that we just might be like a fig tree that is bearing no fruit. The good news is that if we are willing to have that pointed out to us, we have the chance to change. A stewardship way of life is not easy and it does not happen overnight. At times, we will find ourselves in need of good gardening tactics involving fertilization and watering. The sad reality is that we live in a world, and even sometimes a church, where accountability is seen as harsh or judgmental. However, we let ourselves and others down by not helping each other see the reality of our actions. Would you want to be that fruitless fig tree that gets cut down without a chance to grow? That would be really harsh. Let's help one another to be the best stewards and disciples we can be.

IDEA FOR RESPONSE

Partner with a friend to hold each other accountable to go to Mass weekly, attend Reconciliation regularly, pray daily.

TAKE TIME TO REFLECT

Have you ever held someone accountable for their behavior? What was their reaction when you did? Did the relationship sour?

FRUIT-BEARING

Wash My Hands (And Feet)

[Jesus] rose from supper and took off his outer garments. He took a towel and tied it around his waist. Then he poured water into a basin and began to wash the disciples' feet and dry them with the towel around his waist. He came to Simon Peter, who said to him, "Master, are you going to wash my feet?" Jesus answered and said to him, "What I am doing, you do not understand now, but you will understand later." Peter said to him, "You will never wash my feet." Jesus answered him, "Unless I wash you, you will have no inheritance with me." Simon Peter said to him, "Master, then not only my feet, but my hands and head as well."

–John 13:4-9

My mother always had me wash my hands before dinner. Even if we hadn't been outside of the house, she still made me march to the sink to wash my hands. She was a bit of a germophobe, but it was a good practice nevertheless. I had to take responsibility for myself and make sure I was acting in a healthy manner. No one was going to wash my hands for me, she often reminded me in commanding me to the faucet.

In our faith lives, however, we cannot wash ourselves clean. No commands from mom or repeated attempts at washing can make us clean and subsequently ready for the banquet God has prepared for us. Jesus not only knelt down to the ground to wash the feet of his apostles because he was leading by example, he washed their feet because they could not do so for themselves. They had prepared themselves for meals many times in the past, but this was no ordinary meal. Preparation for this meal would take more than the power bestowed to humans. It would take a divine power.

After he was done, he said to his apostles, "If I, therefore, the master and teacher, have washed your feet, you ought to wash one another's feet. I have given you a model to follow, so that as I have done for you, you should also do." We cannot live this faith in isolation. We must prepare one another. We must wash the feet of one another. My mom said no one was going to wash my hands for me, but I pray someone will be willing to wash my feet.

IDEA FOR RESPONSE

Reach out to a parishioner in need. Offer to include them in your prayers or have a Mass said for them.

TAKE TIME TO REFLECT

Name 3 times when people in your parish community have given you comfort and support. How did you show your gratitude?

COMMUNITY

God Only Knows

The word of the LORD came to me:
Before I formed you in the womb I knew you,
  before you were born I dedicated you,
  a prophet to the nations I appointed you.
"Ah, Lord GOD!" I said,
  "I do not know how to speak. I am too young!"
But the LORD answered me,
Do not say, "I am too young."
  To whomever I send you, you shall go;
  whatever I command you, you shall speak.

–Jeremiah 1:4-7

When my wife was pregnant with our first child, I remember putting headphones on her stomach and playing classical music and the Beach Boys so my unborn child could develop a love for music. Some say such an action can work. Others say I was nuts. Either way, I don't care because I was forming a bond with my child before I even really knew him. When my first son was born, he didn't start singing "Good Vibrations," but it was as if we already had some form of communication going on between us.

The Lord said to Jeremiah, "Before I formed you in the womb I knew you, before you were born I dedicated you, a prophet to the nations I appointed you." God knew Jeremiah, and He knew us, even before we were born. I was interacting on some level with my unborn son, but I didn't really know him. I didn't know he would be born with curly hair. I didn't know that as he grew he would have a natural talent with math. I didn't know he would feel uncomfortable in front of a group or that he would be a fast runner. None of these things did I know about my son, but God knew it all. For even though my son was result of the love between my wife and me, I did not create my son. God created him. And then this person whom He created and knew inside and out was given to my wife and me as gift.

I pray every day that my son might grow ever closer to his heavenly Father. I don't want him to drift away from me, but I want us to draw ever closer to God together. This is being a good steward with my children. I hope to one day hear my son sing a new song unto the Lord, even if it was not recorded by the Beach Boys.

IDEA FOR RESPONSE

Spend 15 minutes in prayer this week asking God to allow you to see yourself as He sees you.

TAKE TIME TO REFLECT

Have you ever felt you weren't ready to be a disciple of Jesus and that you are still too immature in your faith?

NOTES

NOTES

NOTES

Scripture Passages

About LPi

Our Mission:

To equip our Catholic Church customers with communication and engagement solutions so they can focus on their mission to evangelize new generations.

Today, the Catholic Church faces challenges from many sides: an ever-increasing secularism, declining numbers of clergy, and the loss of too many young people. At LPi, our goal is to equip parishes and dioceses with the tools needed to lead people to a more intentional discipleship and an Everyday Stewardship way of life.

We produce products that drive stewardship and engagement and also assist communities in more clearly and boldly proclaiming the Good News. Our experienced staff is always ready to help you implement these tools and to share with you the innovative and effective best practices we have learned from our 45 years of working in and with our 6,000+ parish partners. We are not just about forward-thinking products — we are part of the Church community.

LPi BECAUSE VIBRANT CHURCHES MATTER

About the Author

Tracy Earl Welliver enjoys long walks on the beach, listening to Yacht Rock, buying vinyl records, playing guitar, and watching movies his family thinks make no sense. He tries to see the good in all things and God's presence all around. Tracy tries to live a stewardship way of life every day but fails miserably often, which provides for constant inspiration for further writings. He lives in Greensboro, North Carolina, with his wife and three children.

Tracy is also a Catholic speaker, author, teacher, and stewardship/strengths coach with over 25 years of experience in ministry. He is currently the Director of Parish Community and Engagement for LPi. Tracy also currently sits on the ICSC Board of Directors. He has a BA in Theology from DeSales University and a MTS from Duke Divinity School.

COACHING & CONSULTING
Stewardship, Strengths & Engagement to Build Your Vibrant Parish

THE EVERYDAY STEWARDSHIP VISION

As the baptized, we are called to grow in our faith to a point where we respond to the call of Jesus Christ regardless of the cost. This leads us to an everyday way of living, not just a series of activities or good deeds. When we find ourselves truly living a stewardship way of life, we realize that we have transformed, to aid in transforming our parishes and then the world around us.

STEWARDSHIP, STRENGTHS & ENGAGEMENT COACHING

Talks & Workshops
Invite Tracy Earl Welliver to speak at your parish or diocese. You can choose topics in engagement, strengths and talents, communication, and Everyday Stewardship.

Parish Missions
Inspire your parishioners with Tracy Earl Welliver speaking at all weekend Masses and leading five additional talks over 2–3 days.

Strengths Coaching
Uncover your God-given talents and work to cultivate them into strengths for God's glory with a Gallup© trained & certified strengths coach during a day or weekend retreat, or individual parish leaders coaching.

Planning & Assessment
Let LPi work with you on a vision or use our assessment tools to uncover what is going on in the community.

Parish Staff Coaching
Use the StrengthsFinder© assessment and solid pastoral ministry principles to help your staff and leadership team learn to work together for the greater good of the parish community.

For more information, contact Tracy Earl Welliver at (800) 950-9952 x2676 or twelliver@4lpi.com or go to 4LPi.com/solutions/coaching-consulting/.